THE

ORIGIN AND SIGNIFICANCE

OF

THE GREAT PYRAMID

BY

C. STANILAND WAKE

AUTHOR OF "THE EVOLUTION OF MORALITY," &c., &c.

LONDON:
REEVES & TURNER, 196, STRAND, W.C.

1882

THE BOOK TREE
SAN DIEGO, CALIFORNIA

Originally published 1882
Reeves &Turner
London

New material and revisions
© 2002, 2024
The Book Tree
All rights reserved

ISBN 978-1-58509-464-6

Cover photo
© Whatafoto

Cover layout
Paul Tice

Published by
The Book Tree
San Diego, CA
www.thebooktree.com

We provide fascinating and educational products to help awaken the public to new ideas and information that would not be available otherwise.
Call 1 (800) 700-8733 for our FREE BOOK TREE CATALOG.

INTRODUCTION

Brought back into print due to its important level of research, this book digs deeper into the mystery of the Great Pyramid than most books found today on the subject. The author had access to references no longer easily found and in most cases, never again used by others. This book connects the Great Pyramid to ancient constellations, cycles of time, the great flood, serpent worship, Sabaism, one specific Egyptian god, and advanced mathematical concepts that explain its purpose and alignment. An earlier edition of this work stated, "A different approach to the problem of the Great Pyramid is presented in this rare volume. Far from being restricted to biblical prophecy, the Great Pyramid is shown to be a timeless representation of the theorem *mathematics is to spirit as geometry is to matter*. He who can unravel the mystery will be shown a system fundamentally apparent in nature—revealing cycles proportions, distance, time, and measures, in relation to man and his world. The Appendix contains the strange fragments from the early Arabian historians Masoudi as well as Makrizi, together with the introduction to Mr. J. Ralston Skinner's *Source of Measures*, added for serious students." Anyone seeking a reasonable explanation for this great wonder of the world should include this book in their search.

Paul Tice

PREFACE

The subject treated of in the following pages has during the last few years attracted much attention, thanks to the influence of Prof. C. Piazzi Smyth's important work, "Life and Work at the Great Pyramid." It was to test, by the light of history, the conclusion accepted by that writer as to the inspired origin of the Great Pyramid that I entered upon a consideration of the subject. That such an origin was required by the facts, I did not suppose, but the conviction was forced on me that the structure had much more importance, viewed as a scientific and religious monument, than was generally conceded. I found nothing, however, to show that either its design or its construction necessitated Divine intervention. I was led to the conclusion, nevertheless, that the builders of the Great Pyramid intended to perpetuate certain scientific ideas, and, moreover, that they had a religious motive in its erection. There is little doubt, indeed, that it is a monument of Sabaism—the worship of the heavenly host, which had a wide extension in the ancient world, and with which "Serpent worship" was intimately connected. The importance of the Great Pyramid as a religico-scientific structure is still further increased if, as is not improbable, it was intended to mark the substitution of an astronomy based on the passage of the sun through the twelve signs of the Zodiac for the lunar astronomy which preceded it. My endeavour has been to state fairly the historical conditions of the problem considered, and to point out the direction in which its solution must be sought. With the question as to the original source from which the wisdom of the Ancients, of which the Great Pyramid is so wonderful a monument, was derived, these pages are not concerned.

The Serpent, enclosed in a pyramid, given on the cover, is taken from a gem figured in Matter's "Histoire Critique du Gnosticism," *planche* II B, figure 2. It is there said to be the Solar Chnouphis or Agathodemon—Christos, with the seven sons of Sophia (Wisdom), the seven planetary genii.

The substance of this little work was read as a Paper before the Hull Literary Club on the 13th March, 1882.

The Sphinx, and the Great Pyramid of Gizeh.

TABLE OF CONTENTS

CHAPTER I

THE ASTRONOMICAL THEORY

CHAPTER II

EARLY EGYPTIAN CIVILIZATION

CHAPTER III

THE TOMB THEORY

CHAPTER IV

THE RELIGIOUS THEORY

CHAPTER V

SETH AND SERPENT WORSHIP

Human skulls unearthed during the excavations of the Temple of the Second Pyramid of Gizeh.

THE

ORIGIN AND SIGNIFICANCE

OF

THE GREAT PYRAMID

CHAPTER I

THE ASTRONOMICAL THEORY

THE GREEKS of the time of Alexander the Great were so impressed with the magnitude or splendour of certain edifices, that they spoke of them as the seven wonders of the world. Among these, the first place was given to the Pyramids of Egypt, and pre-eminently to those of Ghizeh, which are situate a few miles from Cairo, and in the neighbourhood of ancient Memphis. The Pyramids of Ghizeh form a group of nine, consisting of three large ones, known as the Pyramid of Cheops, or the Great Pyramid; that of Cephren; and that of Mycerinus, which is inferior in size to either of the others. The six other pyramids of the Ghizeh group are much smaller, and are supposed to be the tombs of female relatives of the kings who constructed the larger ones. From the term "Great" applied to the largest pyramid, it might be thought that it far exceeds in size any of the others. As a fact, however, the Pyramid of Cephren is not very much smaller than that of Cheops, which was about 756 feet square at the base and 480 feet high, as against 707 feet 9 inches the extreme length of the sides, and 454 the height, of the Second Pyramid. Moreover, the construction of the two pyramids was, according to Col. Vyse, carried on upon the same principles. This is true more especially of the general design and external characters of the buildings, which in their internal features, however, differ considerably.* The position of the chambers, and the inclination of the passages of the Great Pyramid are exceptional, and, judging from these peculiarities and from certain scientific facts supposed to be embodied in it, several modern writers have affirmed that the design for the Great Pyramid must have been derived from an inspired source. The originator of this theory was John Taylor who in 1859, published a book on the subject

* "The Great Pyramid: Why was it built? and who built it?"

and as in recent years it has attracted considerable attention, chiefly through its adoption by the author of "Life and Work at the Great Pyramid," Prof. C. Piazzi Smyth, the Astronomer Royal of Scotland, and as the scientific facts on which it is based are admittedly true, it is necessary to consider the theory.

In the first place, the Great Pyramid is said to embody in its form and proportions certain facts as to the size and shape of the earth. Thus, John Taylor says that the builders of the Great Pyramid "imagined the earth to be a sphere, and as they knew that the radius of a circle must bear a certain proportion to its circumference, they built a four-sided pyramid of such a height in proportion to its base that its perpendicular would be the radius of a sphere equal to the perimeter of the base." This shape is supposed to have reference to an important astronomical fact, seeing that "the vertical height of the Great Pyramid multiplied by 10 to the 9th power (10^9) tells the mean distance of the sun from the earth—that is, one thousand million times the pyramid's height, or 91,840,000 miles." * More-

* Mr. Proctor regards this fact as a mere coincidence, although he deems it probable that the smaller unit of measurement used

over, the Great Pyramid is thought to supply a standard of linear measure, based on the length of the polar axis of the earth. Assuming this length to be 500,500,000 of our inches, the 500 millionth of that axis (omitting fractions) will be one inch. Of these inches, 25 or 25·025 of our inches would form a cubit or longer standard, the ten millionth part of the semi-axis of the globe in length, which is the measure of the sacred cubit of the ancient Hebrews. This cubit of 25 earth inches is contained in each side of the Great Pyramid as many times as there are days in the year, and the inch itself "is contained separately and independently in the entire perimeter of the Great Pyramid's base just one hundred times for each day of the year." The inch is also said to be the "representative of a year in the reckoning of the passage floor lines as charts of history, also in the diagonals of the pyramid's base taken as a measure of the precessional cycle."

The Great Pyramid is found, moreover, to furnish an important weight and capacity mea-

by the Great Pyramid builders was intended to have a relation to the earth's diameter, as stated in the text.—"Myths and Marvels of Astronomy" (Ed. 1880), pp. 66, 73.

sure having relation to the mean density or specific gravity of the earth. These earth-measures are said to be reproduced in the Coffer preserved in the large or so-called King's Chamber of the Great Pyramid, the internal capacity of which vessel is just four times the measure of an English *quarter* of wheat. The Great Pyramid was thus, according to the holders of the inspiration theory, originally designed as a perfect and complete metrological monument. This conclusion is thought to be supported by the great astronomical knowledge possessed by the builders, who were aware, not only of the shape and rotatory motion of the earth, but also of its distance from the sun. They were able, further, to do what was found so difficult up to a comparatively recent date—to fix with precision the position of the four cardinal points, as is shewn by the fact that the pyramid stands due North, South, East, and West.

The Great Pyramid is thus seen to be an important *astronomical* monument, and it is no less remarkable in relation to certain *chronological* facts. It is supposed to perpetuate the great cycle founded on the precession of the equinoxes. This siderial year is equal to 25,868 of our years, and the two diagonals of the pyramid's base taken together are said to measure just the same number of inches. It is thought, moreover, that by means of this cycle the date of the erection of the pyramid can be ascertained. Assuming that the long narrow downward passage leading from the entrance was directed towards the pole star of the pyramid builders, astronomers have shown that in the year 2,170 B.C. the passage pointed to Alpha Draconis, the then pole star, at its lower culmination, at the same time that the Pleiades, particularly Alcyone, the centre of the group, were on the same meridian above. This relative position of Alpha Draconis and Alcyone being an extraordinary one, as it could not occur again for a whole siderial year, it is thought to mark the date of the building of the Great Pyramid.* It should be mentioned, however, that the date named is not the only possible one. Mr. Richard A. Proctor the astronomer, after stating that the Pole-star was in the required position about 3,350 B.C., as well as in 2,170 B.C., says "either of

* I have taken the opinions of the Pyramidalists from the 9th edition of an ingenious work by Dr. Seiss, of Philadelphia, entitled "A Miracle in Stone."

these would correspond with the position of the descending passage in the Great Pyramid; but Egyptologists tell us there can absolutely be no doubt that the later epoch is far too late." He adds: "If then we regard the slant passage as intended to bear on the Pole-star at its sub-polar passage, we get the date of the pyramid assigned as about 3,350 years B.C., with a probable limit of error of not more than 200 years either way, and perhaps of only fifty years."*

The testimony of Mr. Proctor is important as he has recently performed very valuable work in pointing out the true astronomical meaning of the passages and galleries which distinguish the internal structure of the Great Pyramid from that of other pyramids. We may now accept the view that the former has been erected with an astronomical purpose, although its measurements may not have all the significance sometimes assigned to them.

Mr. Proctor, while admitting the existence of many of the curious coincidences on which the theory of the inspired origin of the Great

* *Knowledge* Vol. i. pp. 242-400. This agrees very well with one of the dates given by Diodorus, but 2,170 B.C. is a preferable date on grounds which will be referred to *infra.*

Pyramid is based, gives an entirely different explanation of them. He declares, indeed, "that they are *mere* coincidences, and that they would still remain if the pyramid had no existence." The fact that they exist, and are in themselves so singular, shows simply how little value there is in the argument from mere coincidence.* In support of this opinion, Mr. Proctor refers to "the multititude of relations, independent of the pyramid, which have turned up while Pyramidalists have been endeavouring to connect the pyramid with the solar system." "These coincidences," he says, "are altogether more curious than any coincidence between the Pyramid and astronomical numbers: the former are as close and remarkable as they are real; the latter, which are only imaginary, have only been established by the process which schoolboys call 'fudging,' and now new measures have left the work to be done all over again."† The new measures here referred to show that the base of the pyramid is

* They must, however, have been more than mere coincidences if the builders of the pyramid had the astronomical knowledge displayed in its perfect orientation and in its other admitted astronomical features. See *infra*.

† See Mr. Petrie's letter to *The Academy*, Dec. 17, 1881. Mr. Proctor's views are taken from *Knowledge*, Vol i. unless otherwise stated.

several feet shorter than had been supposed, and this will necessitate a change in the pyramid inch and in the length of the cubit on which the astronomical relations of the Great Pyramid were based.

Mr. Proctor's own explanation of the peculiar features which distinguish the internal construction of the Great Pyramid from that of the other pyramids is very ingenious, and probably conclusive: He says, we see "in all the Egyptian pyramids the evidence of an astronomical plan; and in the Great Pyramid we find evidence that such a plan was carried out with great skill, and with an attention to points of detail which shows that, for some reason or other, the edifice was required to be most carefully built in a special astronomical position." Moreover, to obtain such accuracy, it was made to serve, while being built, "the purpose of an astronomical observatory." To this end, "the builders of the Great Pyramid used the passages which they made within it to determine the proper position of each part of it, up to the so-called King's Chamber, at least, and probably higher." The slant descending passage was directed to the position of the Pole-star when it was due north and at its lowest, for the purpose of obtaining true orientation. As layer after layer of the building was placed, this passage was carried towards the north until it reached the northern face of the Pyramid. Here it was compelled to terminate and another mode of observing the Pole-star had to be used. This was effected by making a fresh passage "in such a direction as to contain the rays from the Pole-star after reflection at a horizontal surface, such as that of still water." The reflecting surface required was obtained by plugging the descending passage and pouring in water so as to partially fill the angle thus formed, from which the rays would be reflected up the ascending passage. Mr. Proctor remarks that thus far the pyramid builders had "been working with manifest reference to the meridional plane, just as an astronomer of our own time would; and it looks very much, even from what we have already seen, as though they had considered this plane for the same reason that the modern astronomer considers it—viz., because this is the plane in which all the heavenly bodies culminate, or attain the middle and highest point of their passage from the eastern to the western horizon." Mr. Proctor adds that at the point where the

Grand Gallery commences all doubt ceases. "The astronomical nature of the builder's purpose becomes here as clear and certain as already the astronomical nature of their methods had been. For from here upwards the small ascending passage is changed to one of great height, so as to command a long vertical space of the heavens, precisely as a modern astronomer sets his transit circle to sweep the vertical meridian." This Grand Gallery shows that it was intended for astronomical observations by its double character. Its walls, taken as wholes, are aslant, but every part of the them is absolutely vertical, as would be required by an astronomer if his observations were to be of value. To facilitate these observations, long slant stone ramps or banks are placed at each side of the gallery the whole of its length, with holes in them at equal distances for the purpose of receiving movable seats. Regarded as a kind of architectural transit instrument, the Great Gallery would, says Mr. Proctor, "have to be carried to a certain height, and there open out on the level to which the pyramid had then attained, the sides and top being carried up until the southernmost end of the gallery was completed." At that end commences the so-called

Antechamber, and the floor of this chamber and of the King's Chamber, then not walled in, would serve to station a time indicator and the watchers "appointed to mark the passage of time in some way, and to note also the instants when the observer or observers in the Great Gallery signalled the beginning or end of transit across the gallery's field of view." Mr. Proctor concludes an interesting chapter on this subject by saying, "if a telescopist of our time will try to plan out a method of determining the declinations and right ascensions of stars (say for the purpose of forming a trustworthy star chart or catalogue), without using a telescope, by using such an observing place as the Great Gallery, he will see how much might be done, so far as equatorial and zodiacal stars were concerned; and they are altogether the most important, even now, and were still more so in the days when the stars in their courses were supposed to rule the fates of men and nations." In a further article, Mr. Proctor gives a view of the Pyramid observatory, showing the object end of the great observing tube. In that article he says, "the astronomers who observed from the Great Pyramid doubtless made many more observations off the meridian than on it. . . . They no doubt often used astrolabes and similar instruments to determine the position of stars, planets, comets, etc., when off the meridian, with reference to stars whose places were already determined by the use of their great meridional instrument. But all those observations were regulated by, and derived their value from, the work done in the Great Ascending Gallery. The modern astronomer sees that this was the only way in which exact observations of the heavenly bodies all over the star-sphere could possibly have been made; and seeing the extreme care, the most marvellous pains, which the astronomers of the Great Pyramid took to secure good meridional work, the astronomer recognizes in them fellow workers."

Mr. Proctor very properly assumes, however, that the builder of the Great Pyramid had something more than a scientific purpose in its erection, something beyond even its use as a tomb. That purpose is to be gathered from the fact that "the astronomy of the time of Cheops was essentially astrology, and astrology a most important part of religion." The Great Pyramid was erected as a place from which the heavenly bodies could be observed, and their movements were observed and studied that Cheops might know what was to happen, and learn the times and seasons which were likely to be fortunate or unfortunate for him or his race. "As an astrological edifice," says Mr. Proctor, "a gigantic horoscope for him and for him only, we can understand its purport, much though we may marvel at the vast expenditure of care, labour, and treasure at which it was erected. Granted full faith in astrology (and we know there was such faith), it was worth while to build even such a structure as the Great Pyramid; just as, granted the ideas of Egyptians about burial, we can understand the erection of so mighty a mass, and all save its special astronomical character. Of no other theory, I venture to say, than that which combines these two strange but most marked characteristics of the Egyptian mind, can this be said."

Mr. Proctor gives a figure, taken from Raphael's "Astrology," representing the ordinary horoscope and its relations to "a horizontal, carefully-oriented square plane surface, such as the top of the pyramid was, with just such direction lines as would naturally be used on such a platform";

and, apart from the reasons assigned by him for the differences in size* between the Pyramids of Cheops, and those of Cephren, his brother, and Mycerinus and Asychis, his son and grandson, Mr. Proctor has conclusively established the astrological purpose of the Great Pyramid. Elsewhere, he says, "remembering the mysterious influence which astrologers ascribed to special numbers, figures, positions, and so forth, the care with which the Great Pyramid was so proportioned as to indicate particular astronomical and mathematical relations is at once explained. The four sides of the square base were carefully placed with reference to the cardinal points, precisely like the four sides of the ordinary square scheme of nativity. The eastern side faced the Ascendant, the southern faced the Mid-heaven, the western faced the Descendant, and the northern faced the Imum Cœli. Again, we can understand that the architects would have made a circuit of the base correspond in length with the number of days in the year—a relation which, according to Prof. P. Smyth, is fulfilled in this manner, that the four sides contain one hundred times as many

* The size of each Pyramid is usually supposed to denote the length of the reign of the Monarch by whom it was constructed.

pyramid inches as there are days in the year. The pyramid inch again is itself mystically connected with astronomical relations, for its length is equal to the five hundred millionth part of the earth's diameter, to a degree of exactness corresponding well with what we might expect Chaldean astronomers to attain. . . . It is not [indeed] at all certain that the sacred cubit bore any reference to the earth's dimensions, but this seems tolerably well made out—that the sacred cubit was about 25 inches in length, and that the circuit of the pyramid's base contained a hundred inches for every day of the year. Relations such as these are precisely what we might expect to find in buildings having an astrological significance. Similarly, it would correspond well with the mysticism of astrology that the pyramid should be so proportioned as to make the height be the radius of a circle whose circumference would equal the circuit of the pyramid's base. Again, that long slant tunnel, leading downwards from the pyramid's northern face, would at once find a meaning in this astrological theory. The slant tunnel pointed to the pole-star of Cheops's time, when due north below the true pole of the heavens. This circumstance had no observational utility. It could afford no indication of time, because a pole-star moves very slowly, and the pole-star of Cheops's day must have been in view through that tunnel for more than an hour at a time. But, apart from the mystical significance which an astrologer would attribute to such a relation, it may be shown that this slant tunnel is precisely what the astrologer would require in order to get the horoscope correctly."* Mr. Proctor supports his view as to the astrological object of the pyramid by reference to the fact that in the account given by Ebn Abd Al Hôkm of the contents of the Pyramids of Ghizeh, those assigned to the East or Great Pyramid "relate entirely to astrology and associated mysteries."† The Arab writer, or rather the earlier historian, Masoudi, whose account he repeats, says, "in the eastern pyramid were inscribed the heavenly spheres, and figures representing the stars and planets in the forms in which they were worshipped. The king also deposited the instruments and the thuribula with which his forefathers had sacrificed to the stars,

* "Myths and Marvels of Astronomy" (Ed. 1880), p. 101.

† Ditto, p. 103.

and their circles; together with the history and chronicles of time past, of that which is to come, and of every future event which would take place in Egypt."*

The connection of astrology with the Great Pyramid is thus confirmed by ancient testimony, but this does not support the notion that the chief object of its erection was astrological. An early Arab writer, Jafer Ben Mohammed Balkhi, who was himself an astrologer, says that the pyramids were built for refuge against an approaching destruction of every created being, by submersion or by fire, which was foreseen by wise men previous to the flood.† The founder of the Great Pyramid had undoubtedly a more permanent object in its erection than its use as a horoscope for the benefit of himself and his family. Mr. Proctor speaks of the religious observances associated with astrological observations. These, being made by priests, were religious in character, and in all probability the priests who made them "professed a religion differing little from pure Sabaism, or the worship

* See Appendix II.

† Vyse, "Operations at the Pyramids of Gizeh," Vol. p. 319.

of the heavenly host," of which astrology was the natural offspring. Religion has here a a secondary character, however, and it is quite subsidiary to the astrological purpose with which the pyramid is supposed to have been erected. The reverse of this would be nearer the truth, and it will be hereafter shown that whatever may have been its temporary purpose, its primary object was religious.

CHAPTER II

EARLY EGYPTIAN CIVILIZATION

NOTWITHSTANDING the religious object of the erection of the Great Pyramid, there is no ground for supposing that its erection required the aid of Divine inspiration or guidance. Prof. Smyth affirms however, that the Great Pyramid measures are quite different from those used by the ancient Egyptians. They were the sacred measures of the Hebrews, but this people could not, according to Prof. Smyth, have been its builders, as they were dwellers in tents. Nor, on the same authority, were the Egyptians more competent. Their wisdom was not sufficient to enable them to design the Great Pyramid. The civilization of the Egyptians, moreover, had a sudden beginning, so that they could not have gradually acquired the necessary scientific knowledge for such a purpose. Prof. Smyth further asserts that there is no evidence of the existence of an earlier race who could have designed the Great Pyramid, and he affirms that it was erected by a people foreign to the land of Egypt, whom he calls Cushites or Chaldeans, under Divine guidance.*

It is evident that the real argument of those who hold the theory of divine inspiration in relation to the Great Pyramid is the supposed absence of any people who could by their own knowledge design the structure. Dr. Seiss, who finds a reference to the pyramid in the Book of Job, says as to this ancient book, "In it we find a familiarity with writing, engraving in stone, mining, metallurgy, building, shipping, natural history, astronomy, and science in general, showing an advanced, organised, and exalted state of society, answering exactly to what pertains above all to the sons of Joktan, whose descendants spread themselves from Upper Arabia to the South Seas, and from the Persian Gulf to the Pillars of Hercules, tracking their course as the first teachers of our modern world with the greatest monuments that antiquity contains."†

* "Life and Work at the Great Pyramid," Vol. iii. pp. 465, *seq.*, 521 *seq*

† "A Miracle in Stone," p. 210.

According to Dr. Seiss, the Joktanites were the true Arabians, and they, and not the Cushites, were the highly cultured people who erected those great monuments. This writer, moreover, sees in Job the son of Joktan, and he suggests the identity of the Patriarch with the Philition, whose name is associated by Herodotus with the erection of the Great Pyramid. It will be thought that as the Joktanites had the scientific qualifications necessary for the erection of the Great Pyramid, there is no occasion to call in the aid of divine inspiration. Not so Dr. Seiss, who terms this great structure "a miracle in stone, a petrifaction of wisdom and truth revealed of God, preserved among his people from the foundation of the world, and thus memorialised by impulse and aid from Him."*

It is evident, however, that Dr. Seiss admits too much. If the Joktanites had the scientific knowledge ascribed to them, they could have built the Great Pyramid without divine guidance. How this knowledge was originally acquired is another question, and one which does not now concern us. Prof. Smyth, who ascribes the building of the pyramid to the influence of the

* "A Miracle in Stone," p. 226.

Cushites, makes an equally fatal admission. He says, "The spirit, then, of the Egyptians at the building of the Great Pyramid was the same which marked them, both at the oppression of the children of Israel afterwards, and, in conjunction with other peoples, at the building of the Tower of Babel before. In so far as the Egyptians could accomplish it in their new work on the banks of the Nile, and as they flattered themselves, too, for ages that they had accomplished it even to the full,—the Great Pyramid was a resurgence in a new land, and with a community speaking a new language, of their thwarted ideas in another place; but through the humble agency of the shepherd Philition their labours were made really to tell against themselves."* The reference made in this passage to the Tower of Babel is important. This building appears to have struck the imagination of the ancient world by its magnitude as much as the Great Pyramid has since done, and we may well suppose that a people who could rear the one could erect the other without supernatural aid. Moreover, if, as Prof. Smyth supposes, the Egyptians sought to carry out in the later

* "Life and Work at the Great Pyramid," Vol. iii. p. 530.

building the ideas which they with other peoples had attempted to embody in the Tower of Babel, there does not appear to be any object in calling in such aid either for the designing or the erection of the Great Pyramid.

It will be objected, however, that the Babylonian Tower could not have formed the model for the great Egyptian edifice, as they were of different construction ; and that, as the Great Pyramid was not only the largest but the earliest of the pyramids, its design could not have been derived from the former through intermediate structures. This argument would doubtless have great force if it were founded on fact. In reality, however, the Pyramids of Ghizeh, although the largest, are not the earliest Egyptian monuments of this description.* The best modern authorities believe that the great Pyramid of Sakkarah was erected by one of the kings of the First Dynasty, whereas the Pyramids of Ghizeh belong to the Fourth Dynasty. If that was so, the fact is of great importance, since the design of the Sakkarah pyramid, as shown by its name of

* Sir J. Gardner Wilkinson ascribes the Pyramid of Abouseir to Shuré (Soris), the immediate predecessor of Cheops, according to Manetho. (*See* Appendix II.)

Pyramid of Degrees, evidently approaches that of the Tower of Babel. It might well have formed the original on which the design of the Great Pyramid of Ghizeh was modelled, notwithstanding that the internal features of the two buildings differ considerably. The peculiarity of the Great Pyramid is that its chambers and passages are chiefly formed in the structure itself, instead of being cut out of the rock on which the building is erected. Sir J. Gardner Wilkinson affirms, indeed, but not very correctly, that the passages of the Second Pyramid are very similar to those of the Great Pyramid; and Prof. Smyth remarks on the analogy between the Sepulchral Room of the one and the so-called King's Chamber of the other structure. This latter authority thinks the analogy not real, however, as the King's Chamber is "140 feet above the ground outside and in the midst of worked masonry, – or in a position where no pyramid was ever yet known to have any chamber or to bury a man; while the large chamber of the Second Pyramid is excavated in rock, and has its floor below the level of the ground outside, – or in a position suitable to burying." The shape and position of the sarcophagus in this burial chamber, as compared with the coffer of the Great Pyramid, are said to weaken still further the analogy, which Prof. Smyth considers to be finally disposed of by the fact, not to be overlooked, that " while the chamber of the Second Pyramid is directly led *to* by the leading of the entrance passage and its conspicuously lined walls, the King's Chamber of the Great Pyramid is just as directly led *away from* by the entrance-passage there, which seems rather to have been a blind and shield to it, and a diversion to all who would come to seek for that remarkable chamber. . . . . Hence *the* chamber in the Great Pyramid, which is truly the representative of the larger one in the Second Pyramid, can be no other than that usually despised, but nevertheless very large, subterranean chamber which is excavated in the rock at the bottom of the long entrance passage, and equally with the chambers excavated in other pyramids must have been intended to be easily discovered, and looked on as sepulchral, while the so-called King's Chamber of the Great Pyramid stands absolutely unique."* From this point of view, it might probably be said that the

* "Life and Work," etc., Vol. i. p. 268.

Great Pyramid was, like other structures of the same kind, intended for a sepulchral monument, but that it had some other aim, denoted by the various chambers and passages which mark its peculiar internal construction. As a fact, however, the subterranean chamber of the Great Pyramid was never completely excavated, from which perhaps may have arisen the tradition that, owing to the opposition of the people, the body of Cheops, the royal builder, was not after all deposited in the tomb prepared for it.

It is only in comparatively modern times that any doubt has been thrown on the sepulchral aim of the Great Pyramid, and we will see what light antiquity throws on the subject. But first as to the period of its erection and the social and political condition which prevailed in Egypt at that epoch. The building of the Pyramids of Ghizeh is universally ascribed to the Fourth Dynasty, and that of the Great Pyramid in particular to Khoufou or Souphis, commonly known as Cheops, the first king of the dynasty. M. Lenormant, in the ninth edition of his important work on the "Ancient History of the East," states, that " the first reigns of the Fourth Dynasty marked the culminating point of the primitive history of Egypt. The splendour and the internal richness of the country would appear to have been immense under these princes, and are sufficiently attested by their prodigious constructions. The limits of the kingdom extended as far as the first cataract; the capital was always at Man-nofri, or Memphis, and the centre of the life of the empire was in its environs."* The Egyptian monarchy was founded by Mena or Menes, who built the royal city of Man-nofri, that is, the "good place," or "good port," and whose dynasty occupied the throne for 253 years. The kings of the Second Dynasty, which probably also belonged to the family of Menes, reigned during a period of 302 years, and it was succeeded by a native Memphite dynasty which endured for 214 years. The Egyptian monarchy had thus existed for more than 750 years before the commencement of the Fourth Dynasty, a period which was amply sufficient for the development of the scientific and artistic knowledge necessary for the construction of even the Great Pyramid itself. An English Egyptologist, Dr. S. Birch, has given a very interesting account of the attainments of Egyptian civilization at that epoch. He says,

* Tom. ii. p. 71.

"Architecture, as represented by the Pyramids, had become an advanced science, and reflected the geometric and theoretical knowledge of mathematics which their form and structure described for all future ages. The technical masonry was unrivalled, the finish admirable and unsurpassed by any later efforts of the Egyptian architect. The hardest materials, such as the granite of Syene, were hewn into the requisite form of the truest proportions, while the softer but more beautiful alabaster had been discovered and worked. In sculpture a canon of proportion had been discovered and laid down for the human figure, and granite, diorite, and other hard stones conquered and moulded into shape by the efforts of the chisel. The statue of Kephren is equal, if not superior, to the subsequent efforts of Egyptian sculpture, while in the features is clearly to be recognised a portrait of the monarch, showing that the power of producing excellent representations of the living form in all its details existed . . . In wood even greater excellence was attained, for in that material the sculptor developed all his power. The wooden statue of the Museum of Boulaq is an unrivalled work of ancient art . . . The bas-reliefs of the tombs are executed with a minute detail . . . The graphic system of writing was complete; the language perfectly represented by the hieroglyphs, which presented to the eye a lively picture on the painted wall of tomb or sepulchre; while the inscriptions show that the religion of the country was already reduced to a system, and the seasons marked by a regular calendar of festivals. The political organization had also attained a considerable degree of refinement. The court of Memphis swarmed with sacerdotal personages, prophets and prophetesses of the gods, and priests attached to the personal worship of the monarch. Scribes and secretaries were attached to the Pharaoh, superintendents were set over every branch of the public service. In private life the Egyptian lord led a charmed life—his estate was cultivated by slaves, his household full of domestics; the barber, the waiting-maid, the nurse, appear as necessary adjuncts to his household as the steward who presided over the distribution and the clerk who checked the expenses of his daily life. Each priest or noble had in his establishment all the trades necessary for his ease and comfort—the glass-blower, the gold-worker, the potter, the tailor, the baker, and the butler. His leisure or *ennui* was charmed by the acrobat and the dancer, the harpist and the singer; games of chance and skill were played either by him or in his presence. The chief occupation of the period, or at all events that most often represented in the tombs, was inspection of the farm." After particularizing the domesticated animals possessed by the noble of the Fourth Dynasty, the food he ate, and the dress he wore, Dr. Birch continues, " Simple, but elegant, furniture ministered to his requirements. Stools, chairs, footstools, couches, and headrests, or wooden pillows—the use of these rests is still retained in Africa,—appear in the furniture of his elegantly-built house . . . He enjoyed all the pleasures of existence, and delighted more in the arts of peace than war."*

This view of early Egyptian society agrees with the statements of other writers. M. Lenormant affirms that the representations on a tomb of one of the great officers under the Third Dynasty show us the Egyptian civilization as completely organized as it was at the date of the conquest by the Persians, or of that by the Macedonians, with a physiognomy perfectly in-

* " Ancient History from the Monuments."—*Egypt*, pp. 42—46.

dividual and the marks of a long anterior existence. The inhabitants of the valley of the Nile had then not only the same species of domestic animals as those which they took with them in their migrations, but certain species of indigenous mammalia which we find only in a savage state, although the only beast of burden is the ass, neither the horse nor the camel being yet known. According to Sir J. Gardner Wilkinson, indeed, the Egyptians of the Fourth Dynasty had "the same settled habits as in later times. We see no primitive mode of life; no barbarous customs; not even the habit, so slowly abandoned by all peoples, of wearing arms when not in military service, nor any archaic art."*

But what was the condition of the Egyptian civilization 750 years earlier, at the commencement of the first Memphite Dynasty? Menes, the founder of the dynasty, is said to have diverted the ancient course of the Nile, and to have constructed a colossal dam to keep back the river, so as to form a site for his capital—a work which still continues to regulate the waters of that region. The city of Memphis with the

* Rawlinson's "Herodotus," vol. ii. p. 344.

neighbouring towns became, says M. Lenormant, quoting M. Maspero, "the home of Egyptian civilization. It was at Memphis that literature developed and flourished; at Memphis, in the palace of the kings, that the exact sciences were cultivated with the greatest care; at Memphis, finally, that the plastic arts produced their *chefs d'œuvre.*" The immediate successor of Menes began the construction of the palace at Memphis, and is reputed to have composed books on medicine.*

The name of the succeeding monarch is given as the constructor of one of the pyramids of Sakkarah. During the reign of the fifth monarch of the dynasty, several chapters of the Book of the Dead are said to have been found, and also a treatise of medicine, of which the text has been preserved to us in the medical papyrus at Berlin. Menes himself is referred to in official history as the perfect type of a monarch, a constructor, a legislator, and a conqueror. The priests, whose power he had broken, represented him as a corrupter of the simplicity of primitive manners, and the introducer of habits of luxury and effeminacy, among them being

* Tom. ii, p. 58.

that of reclining on a bed or couch at meals.* To one of his successors, the second king of the Second Dynasty, is ascribed the erection of the Great Pyramid of Sakkarah, known as the Pyramid of Degrees, which must have long preceded the larger structure at Ghizeh. The form, and especially the underground arrangement of the former structure, are evidence of its great antitiquity, as they reproduce many of the features of the Egyptian tombs of the early Memphite period. These consist of a deep pit, leading to an underground chamber, and surmounted by a building which serves in great measure to conceal the entrance to the proper tomb. The Pyramid of Degrees is formed of a series of such buildings of decreasing size, placed one above the other, the ground beneath it being excavated in various places, so as to form numerous passages and chambers to be used for sepulchral purposes. The same general plan is found in the Second Pyramid of Ghizeh, but in the latter the deep pit is replaced by the long slanting passage.

The civilization which found its home at Memphis might thus well have originated the

* Tom. ii. p. 58, *seq.*

science necessary for the formation of the Great Pyramid. The erection of this building is, indeed, supposed by M. Lenormant to have been preceded several centuries by that of the Sphinx, the image of the reclining Sun-god, and also of the neighbouring temple, the structure of which is described as prodigious even by the side of the Pyramids. An inscription of the time of Khoufou, or Cheops,* speaks of this temple as having been accidentally discovered buried in the sand of the desert, and the Sphinx appears to have had need of repair during the reign of the same monarch. But we cannot suppose the civilization of the founders of Memphis to have been suddenly acquired. The overthrow of the priestly power, which Menes accomplished, requires the prior existence of a culture differing perhaps little, except in its milder and more peaceful character, from that which afterwards developed itself in the Memphite region. Sir J. Gardner Wilkinson, says, indeed, that all the facts lead to the conclusion that the Egyptians had already "made very great progress in the arts of civilization be-

* It should be mentioned, however, that Egyptologists are not agreed in supposing this inscription to be contemporaneous with Cheops.

fore the age of Menes, and perhaps before they immigrated into the valley of the Nile."*

Menes himself was a native of Teni, or Thinis, the chief city of that part of Upper Egypt in which the priestly authority had established its supremacy. In this region numerous cities existed before the foundation of Memphis. "It was," says Lenormant, "the country of the great prehistoric sanctuaries, seats of the sacerdotal dominion, which played the most important part in the origin of civilization." The people themselves were known as Schesou-Hor, "the servants of Horus," the national god *par excellence* of the Egyptian people, and after death they were said to become the conductors of the bark of the Sun in his celestial voyage, and the cultivators of the happy fields of the other life. M. Maspero affirms, that to this prehistoric race "belongs the honour of having constituted Egypt, such as we know it, from the commencement of the historic period. At first divided into a great number of tribes, they commenced by establishing at several points small independent states, each of which had its own laws and worship." They founded

* Rawlinson's "Herodotus," Vol. ii. p. 345.

the principal cities of Egypt and established the most important sanctuaries. These primitive inhabitants of the Nile valley may have been less highly cultured than their descendants of the Great Pyramid epoch, but as they possessed the hieroglyphic form of writing special to the Egyptians, they must have been already considerably advanced in civilization. M. Maspero supposes, that when they first settled in Egypt, the sands of the desert covered all the soil which was not affected by the yearly inundation of the Nile. He adds, however, that "little by little, the new comers learnt to regulate the course of the river, to embank it, to carry by means of irrigating canals fertility into the most distant corners of the valley. Egypt rose from the waters, and became in the hand of man one of the countries the best adapted to the peaceable development of a great civilization." *

* Lenormant, Tom. ii. p. 51, *seq.*

CHAPTER III.

THE TOMB THEORY.

DURING how many centuries before the foundation of the monarchy by Menes the Egyptian culture had been developing, we do not know, but we cannot doubt that under Cheops it was well able to give origin to the Great Pyramid, the construction of which must be regarded as the chief glory of his reign. We have now to consider, from the testimony of ancient writers, what was the object of that gigantic structure. From the inscriptions, it would seem to have been called "the Great Temple of Shofo," and with its precinct to have been dedicated at one time to the worship of that king. We are, however, dependent entirely on the Greek writers for any account of its construction. Herodotus, who lived in the 5th century before Christ, states that the founder of the Great Pyramid, Cheops, was a prince whose crimes and tyranny rendered his name odious, even to posterity. He closed all the temples and forbade the Egyptians to perform sacrifices; after which he made them all work for him. Some were employed to cut stones in the quarries of the so-called Arabian Hills, on the east side of the Nile, and to convey them to the other side of the river, whence the stones were dragged to the Libyan hills; 100,000 men were thus employed at a time, and they were relieved by an equal number every three months. The construction of the causeway for the transport of the stones occupied ten years, which was exclusive of the time spent in levelling the hill on which the Pyramids stand, and in making the subterranean chambers intended for the tomb. The building of the pyramid itself occupied twenty years. After describing the mode of construction, Herodotus states that on the exterior was engraved in Egyptian characters the sum expended in supplying the workmen with food, amounting to 1,600 talents, equal to £200,000 sterling. After other statements, the historian continues, "Cheops, having reigned 50 years, died, and was succeeded by his brother Cephren, who followed the example of his predecessor. Among other monuments he also built a pyramid, but much less in size than that of Cheops. . . . It has neither underground chambers nor any canal flowing into it from the Nile, like the other, where the tomb of its founder is placed in an island surrounded by water." * The Greek writer adds that the priests informed him that Cephren reigned 56 years, so that "the Egyptians were overwhelmed for 106 years with every kind of oppression, and the temples continued to be closed during the whole time. Indeed, they have such an aversion for the memory of these two princes that they will not even mention their names, and for this reason they call the Pyramids after the shepherd Philitis, who at the time of their erection used to feed his flocks near this spot." Herodotus concludes by referring to the erection of the Third Pyramid, which he ascribes to Mycerinus, the son of Cheops. This monarch, disapproving of the conduct of his father, "ordered the temples to be opened, and permitted the people, who had been oppressed by a long series of cruelties, to

* In connection with this statement it may be remarked, that from ancient inscriptions it appears that during the reign of Amenemha III. of the Twelfth Dynasty, the average height of the inundations from the Nile was 24 feet greater than at present. (*See* Dunckers's "History of Antiquity," Vol. i. p. 105.)

return to their work and their religious duties; and administering justice with great equity, he was looked upon by the Egyptians as superior to all the kings who had ever ruled the country."

The next Greek writer whose description of the pyramids of Ghizeh is preserved to us, is Diodorus, who lived about the beginning of the Christian era. He gives the name Chemmis, or Chembis, as that of the builder of the Great Pyramid, which had lasted to his time at least 1,000 years, or "as some say, upwards of 3,400 years," and the whole structure was then uninjured. The building, he says, was by means of mounds (inclined planes), machines not having yet been invented. In this statement he differs from Herodotus, whose account is not otherwise contradicted. After referring to the erection of the Second Pyramid by Cephren, Diodorus says: "Of the two kings who raised these monuments for themselves, neither one nor the other was destined to be buried therein. The people who had endured so much fatigue in building them, and had been oppressed by their cruelty and violence, threatened to drag their bodies from their tombs and tear them to pieces, so that these princes at their death ordered their friends to bury them privately in some other secret place." Strabo, writing at about the same date, remarks that the pyramids were the sepulchres of kings, and he adds, what is not mentioned by the earlier writers quoted, that "near the centre of the sides is a stone which can be taken out, from which a passage leads to the tomb." Finally, Pliny the Roman historian, who lived about 100 years later, refers to the Egyptian pyramids, which he describes as being an "idle and silly display of royal wealth." The three largest pyramids he affirms were all built in 68 years and 4 months. He refers to the supposed use of mounds in their erection, but as these had disappeared he mentions another suggestion, that bridges were made of mud bricks, which, when the work was completed, were used to build private houses. Pliny adds to the details given by other writers, that within the Great Pyramid is a well 86 cubits (129 feet) deep.

It is evident from the agreement of the descriptions given by Herodotus and other Greek writers with the facts, that they must have derived them from well-informed sources. The entrance to the Great Pyramid mentioned by Strabo, near the centre of the side, was discovered by Col. Vyse, and the well referred to by Pliny is a remarkable feature of the building. No excavation or structure answering to the subterranean chamber upon an island surrounded by water from the Nile described by Herodotus, has yet been discovered, but Col. Vyse seemed to think nevertheless that it actually exists. The outer casing of the Great Pyramid having been removed, the inscription in the Egyptian character seen by Herodotus must have disappeared, but those modern writers who ascribe the erection of that structure to divine inspiration suppose it to have been unique in being entirely without inscriptions. The statement of Herodotus is, however, confirmed by various Arab authors, who, according to Dr. Sprenger, "have given the same accounts of the Pyramids, with little or no variation, for above 1000 years." It appears from Masoudi, one of the earliest of these authors, that the pyramids were covered with continuous inscriptions, and he relates the Coptic tradition that the builder ordered the prophecies of the priests to be inscribed on columns and upon the large stones of the pyramids, and written accounts of their wisdom and acquirements in arts and sciences to be depicted on them.* It is impossible now to ascertain how far this statement was correct, but Col. Vyse found the cartouche of Cheops (Suphis) in the rubbish near the Great Pyramid, and recently a piece of the casing has been discovered showing remains of a Greek inscription, which is the more valuable as, says the discoverer, "nothing besides a few fragments with single letters had been previously discovered of the many inscriptions that existed on the casing." †

As the accounts given by the ancient Greek writers are true in so many particulars, we cannot doubt that they have correctly reported what they had heard as to the object with which the Pyramids were erected. They all agree in declaring them to be the tombs of the kings by whom they had been built, although, according to Diodorus, the Egyptian priests asserted that neither Cheops nor Cephren were actually buried in the pyramids which are ascribed to them. That this story was an invention, however, may be assumed from its not being mentioned by

* Vyse, Vol. ii., 324—S.

† Mr. Petrie's letter in *The Academy.* M. de Sacy refers with approval to the statements of Abd Allatif and other Arab writers, that the surfaces of the two great pyramids were covered with inscriptions. (*See* Vyse, Vol ii. p. 342).

Herodotus, although he refers to the aversion which the Egyptians had for the memory of those kings, and accounts for it by their oppressive conduct, and the closing of the temples during the continuance of their reigns. If the sacred places were actually closed, we should have a sufficient reason for the hatred of the memory of Cheops and Cephren exhibited by the Egyptian priests; a hatred which led them afterwards to declare that the people would not allow their bodies to be deposited in the monuments prepared for them.

It has been often pointed out that it is extremely improbable Cephren would have been at the trouble and expense of erecting a gigantic pyramid for his tomb if the body of his predecessor, Cheops, had not been deposited in the pyramid tomb prepared for its reception. There is some reason to believe, however, that these two monarchs, who were brothers, reigned during the same period, a warrant for which belief is found in the statement of Pliny that the three largest pyramids were all erected in 68 years and 4 months.* It is possible, indeed, that the priests

* Wilkinson says that the Great Pyramid was built by Suphis I. (Cheops), and his brother Suphis II. (Num Shufu), while Cephren (Shafra of the Fifth Dynasty), was the founder of the Second Pyramid.—Rawlinson's "Herodotus," Vol. ii. p. 346.

knew of the absence of any corpse, not only from the rock-cut chamber, but also from the coffer in the so-called King's Chamber, and that they invented the story of the people's hatred to account for such absence. Some ground for the belief in the irreligion of Cheops and Cephren may perhaps be found in the fact that their names were not preceded by that of Osiris, as was the case with their successor Mycerinus.* "Among the ancient Egyptians, the departed soul," says Dr. Ebers, "if it were found pure and faithful, became absolutely one with the universal soul whence it was derived, and received the same name, Osiris."† It is true that Dr. Ebers denies that Cheops and Cephren were wicked contemners of the god, on the ground that "as long as Egypt was governed by independent sovereigns, there were prophets or priests of the Osirian or deceased Cheops,‡ and of the other principal pyramid builders, who conducted the worship in the fallen temple of Isis, and who

* Vyse, Vol. ii. p. 95. Dr. Birch says that the coffin of this monarch marks a new religious development in the annals of Egypt.—"Egypt," p. 41.

† "Egypt," Vol. ii., p. 132.

‡ A religious work, called "The Sacred Book," was ascribed to him by the Greek writers.

usually belonged to the oldest families of Memphis." This is consistent, however, with the fact of the deceased monarchs having worshipped a "strange" god and given him priority over Osiris, which would be sufficient to stamp them in the eyes of the orthodox priests as enemies of the Gods of Egypt.

But is there any evidence besides the statements of Greek writers that the Great Pyramid was really used as the tomb of Cheops or any other person? That it was thus used, might perhaps be inferred from the fact, sometimes forgotten, that it is situate in a vast necropolis. M. Perrot in his "Histoire de l'Art," remarks that "the nobles of Egypt, all those who had assisted in the work of the monarchy and received a reflection of its glory, grouped themselves as near as possible around the prince they had served. Distributed thus by reigns and quarters, the private tombs lie close together, all furnished with steles which preserve the name of the dead, most of them ornamented with bas-reliefs painted in brilliant colours, some even decorated with statues placed before their façade."* We know that the smallest

* Tom. i. p. 244. Abd Allatif mentions that there were formerly at Ghizeh a considerable number of small pyramids,

of the three Great Pyramids was the tomb of its builder Mycerinus or Men-ke-ra, as Col. Vyse found in the burial chamber a basalt sarcophagus, with the lid of its wooden coffin having on it in hieroplyphs an address to the deceased monarch, as identified with Osiris.* Vyse states that great precautions had been taken to conceal the position of the sarcophagus, and he doubted whether the real tombs had been discovered in the two larger pyramids.† He adds that the three larger pyramids were all intended for the same purpose, and their construction was carried on upon the same principles. The sarcophagus of the Second Pyramid has no inscription, and is, according toBelzoni, not larger than is necessary for the wooden case of an embalmed human body.‡ It is true that a piece of bone, supposed to be that of an ox, was found in this sarcophagus, but it may not have had anything to do with the original burial, as the Arab writers say nothing apparently of the discovery

which were destroyed by Karakousch, an Emir in the army of Salaheddin Youssef, to supply materials for the building of the walls and citadel of Cairo. (*See* Vyse, "Operations" etc., Vol. ii. p. 336.)

* Tom. i., Vol. ii. p. 94.

† Ditto, p. 104.

‡ Ditto, p. 298.

in this pyramid of any human or other remains, when it was opened by their countrymen. As to the Great Pyramid, if we are to believe those writers, an embalmed human body was actually discovered in the so-called King's Chamber when it was opened by the Caliph Mamoon. This is said to have taken place in the year 820 A.D., and the Arab historian, Abd-el-Hôkm, relates that "a statue resembling a man was found in the sarcophagus, and in the statue (mummy case) was a body with a breastplate of gold and jewels, bearing characters written with a pen which no one understood."* Alkaisi gives much the same story, and he adds that the case stood at the door of the king's palace at Cairo in the year 511—that is, 1133 A.D.† It may be doubted, however, whether this had anything to do with the Great Pyramid. Dr. Ebers mentions that in the middle of the 15th century, "an Emir caused the destuction of the much admired 'green shrine,' which was formed out of a single block of a stone as hard as iron, and ornamented with figures and inscriptions. It was smashed to pieces." He adds, "the golden statue, with

* Wilkinson's "Hand-Book (Egypt)," p 168

† Vyse, Vol. ii. p. 333

eyes of precious stones, which had once been enshrined in this marvel of art—dedicated probably to the Moon-god Chonsu—had long before disappeared.* In this shrine and statue we have no doubt the case and body mentioned by Abd-el-Hôkm, as Alkaisi when referring to these speaks of an image of a man in green-stone, containing a body in golden armour with a large ruby overhead.

It must be admitted, therefore, that there is no reliable evidence of any human body having been found in the Great Pyramid. Nevertheless this is not any proof that the building was *not* used as a tomb. The Arab writer Abd Allatif refers to an early statement that when the Persians conquered Egypt they took away great riches from the Pyramids, which were the sepulchres of the kings,† and, therefore, no doubt the receptacle of their treasures. Moreover, according to Sir Gardner Wilkinson, the Egyptians themselves had in many instances plundered the tombs of Thebes,‡ and he seems to think that the Great Pyramid met with the same fate at their hands.

* "Egypt" (Eng. Ed.), Vol. i. p. 125.

† Vyse, Vol. ii. p. 345.

‡ "Hand-Book (Egypt)," p. 168.

The Meydoom Pyramid, which is said to be that of the last king of the Third Dynasty, has been recently opened, and inscriptions have been found showing that it had been opened before the Twentieth Dynasty.* M. Lenormant states that the priestly legend as to the popular hatred of the builders of the two Great Pyramids, had at least a real historical foundation. He says: "Everything seems to indicate that the end of the Fourth Dynasty, immediately after the princes constructors of the great pyramids, was a time of revolutions and of troubles caused by the preceeding oppression.† The comparison of the list of Manetho and of the monuments of the necropolis of Sakkarah reveal during this period violent competitions. The splendid statues of Kha-f-Râ (Cephren) in diorite, in rose granite, in alabaster, and in basalt, which decorated the temple near the Great Sphinx, have been found in pieces in a well where they had been precipitated in a revolutionary movement, evidently but little posterior to his reign. These statues,

* Miss Amelia B. Edwards, *The Academy* for Jan. 7th, 1882.

† May there not have been a religious cause, connected with a difference of race, such as the opposition, hereafter referred to, between Seth and Osiris?

moreover, of which some represent him in the vigour of manhood, and the others in a state of advanced age, confirm the tradition which attributed to him a reign of 50 years."* Remains of this character have not yet been found in association with the Great Pyramid, notwithstanding the tradition as to its being the tomb of Cheops, and the fact that it became dedicated to his worship.

It is not at all improbable that the bodies of both Cephren and Cheops were removed from their resting places during the commotions which occurred at the end of the Fourth Dynasty. As to the latter monarch, at least, it is not necessary to suppose that he was buried in the so-called King's Chamber or in the cave below the base of the pyramid. A more likely place for the purpose would be the niche in the east wall of the Queen's Chamber, where Maillet,† who in 1692 described it as being three feet deep, eight feet high, and three feet wide, supposed the mummy of the queen to have been placed upright. The niche appears, however, to have an inner shelf, on which the embalmed corpse may have been

* Tom ii. p. 73.

† Vyse, "Operations," etc., Vol. ii. p. 226.

laid. The Queen's Chamber is stated, however, by Edrysy* to have had an empty "vessel," such as the sarcophagus of the King's Chamber, so that if the niche were used for another purpose the body of Cheops may still have been there deposited. It appears, indeed, that according to some ancient inscriptions, the Pyramids were regarded as sepulchral temples, and priests were appointed for the service of the princes who were buried there, and had attained to the divine nature. A tomb found at Sakkarah belonged to "a priest of Chufu and Chafra."†

* Vyse, Vol. ii. p. 334. May not the Eighth Pyramid, which tradition assigns as the tomb of the daughter of Cheops, have been that of his wife? The masonry has much resemblance to that of the Great Pyramid. Vol. ii. p. 70.

† Duncker, "History of Antiquity," Vol. i. p. 99.

CHAPTER IV.

THE RELIGIOUS THEORY.

THE Great Pyramid was intended to be something more than the tomb or even a temple in honour of Cheops. The astronomical character of many of the chief features of the structure confirms this view, and it is supported by the arguments used by Mr. Proctor to establish its connection with astrological observances. The pyramid had, indeed, a religious character of its own, which probably supplied the primary object of its erection. It is true that Mr. Proctor remarks that it is not "easy to understand why any building at all, except an astronomical observatory, should be placed so that its four faces front the four cardinal points." He says, however, that "a temple devoted to Sun-worship, and generally to the heavenly bodies, might be built in that way. For it is to be noticed that the peculiar figure and position of the Pyramids would bring about the following relations : when the sun rose and set south of the east and west points, or (speaking generally) between the autumn and the spring equinoxes, the rays of the rising and setting sun illuminated the southern face of the pyramid ; whereas, during the rest of the year, that is, during the six months between the spring and autumn equinoxes, the rays of the rising and setting sun illuminated the northern face. Again, all the year round the sun's rays passed from the eastern to the western face at solar noon. And, lastly, during seven months and a half of each year, namely, for three months and three quarters before and after Midsummer, the noon rays of the sun fell on all four faces of the pyramid, or, according to a Peruvian expression (so Smyth avers) the sun shone on the pyramid 'with all his rays.'" Such conditions as these might have been regarded as very suitable for a temple devoted to Sun-worship. And yet Mr. Proctor declares that the temple theory is as untenable as the tomb theory, on the ground, first, that the pyramid form is unsuited for all "the ordinary requirements of a temple of worship," and, secondly, that it gives no explanation of the fact that each king built a pyramid, and each king only one.*

These objections would, however, present no difficulty if the temple theory were restricted to the Great Pyramid, the other pyramids being probably intended only for the tombs of their founders. That the erection of the former had a distinctly religious purpose can hardly be denied. What that purpose was may be gathered from the statements of certain Arab writers. Thus Soyuti mentions from earlier writers that the Sabæans made pilgrimages to the Pyramids and had opened one of them, and that they sacrificed hens and black calves, and burnt incense. He says also that Seth took possession of Egypt, and his son was Hermes, and that he introduced Sabaism, which inculcated, among other things, a pilgrimage to the Pyramids. He adds that, according to some accounts, one pyramid is the tomb of Seth.† An earlier writer, Eddin Ahmed Ben Yahya, does not refer to Seth, but he says that each pyramid was consecrated to a star, and that the Sabæans performed religious pilgrimages to the greatest

* "Myths and Marvels of Astronomy," p. 89.

† See Vyse, "Operations," etc., Vol. ii. p. 358.

and also visited the others. He observes that every pyramid presents the form of a lantern surrounded by equilateral sides, which indicates that it was sacred to a star.* Abd Allatif, who wrote nearly 200 years earlier, also refers to the pilgrimages made to the Pyramids, and he affirms that he had read in ancient Sabæan books that one pyramid was the tomb of Agathodæmon, and the other of Hermes.† Agathodæmon was none other than Seth, and according to some writers Hermes was his son.‡

A modern author, Mr. Palgrave, states that frequent enquiries were made of him in Oman regarding the Egyptian Pyramids, a memory, he thinks, derived from old Sabæan times.§ This traveller remarks elsewhere that the Arab writers give us the following information as to the ancient Sabæans. "That they worshipped the seven planets, and pre-eminently the sun; that they observed a fast of thirty days, set apart in the early spring, before the vernal

* Vyse, "Operations," Vol. ii. p. 349. According to the Platonists, a pyramid is the *figure* of fire.

† Vyse, vol. ii., p. 342.

‡ See Appendix I. for various ancient references to Seth and Hermes, as given by Dr. Sprenger.

§ Vol. ii. p. 264.

equinox; that their chief annual feast coincided with the entrance of the sun in the sign of Aries (a fact which supposes a solar, not lunar, computation of the months); that they had a special veneration for the two great pyramids of Egypt, believed by them to be the sepulchres of Seth and Idrus (Enoch); that their stated prayers recurred seven times a day . . . . and that during their devotions they turned their faces towards the north; lastly, that they possessed a book, or code of laws, ascribed to Seth himself (in what language, unhappily, it is not said), and believed to contain the dogmas and institutions of that primeval patriarch." Mr. Palgrave adds, that two points of great importance seem to have distinguished the ancient form of Sabaism: one, the absence of image-idols and idolatry; the other, the absence of any priestly caste.* These points are, indeed, of great importance, and if it can be shown that the two great pyramids had really anything to do with Sabaism, it is not surprising that their founders were regarded with hatred by the Egyptian priests. The builder of the Third Pyramid, Mycerinus, was not so regarded, however, and

* Vyse, vol. ii. p. 258.

perhaps, therefore, he may be referred to in the legend which spoke of one of the pyramids of Ghizeh as the tomb of Hermes. This personage was not only the son of Seth, but probably also the same as Thoth, the Egyptian god of Wisdom; and to the reign of Mycerinus was assigned the discovery of a mystical text, which formed the most profound passage in the Book of the Dead. M. Lenormant states that numerous legends of the discoveries of books of a supernatural and divine origin were current among the Egyptians, who generally placed them under the earliest dynasties.*

We have already had occasion to notice that the city of Memphis, near which the Pyramids were situated, was founded by Menes, who established a political and military monarchy on the ruins of the priestly authority. Prior to his reign, the priests had exercised supreme power, the chief seat of which was in the middle part of Upper Egypt. In this region, says Lenormant, was situate Abydos, the principal centre of the worship of Osiris, whose tomb was there shown, the only worship which was common to all Egypt; Thebes, which boasted itself to have

* "Histoire Ancienne de l'Orient," 9th edition, Tom. ii. p. 74.

been the birth-place of the same god ; Tentyris, the favorite abode of the goddess Hathor; Deb or Edfou, where Har-m-akhouti, with his son Har-houd, are supposed to have assembled the army with which they combatted Set or Typhon.* Set or Seth is thus brought into connection with the Egyptian mythology, and he occupies a remarkable position in relation to it. "Seth was at one time," says Bunsen, "a great god, universally adored throughout Egypt, who conferred on the sovereigns of the Eighteenth and Nineteenth Dynasties the symbols of life and power. The most glorious monarch of the latter dynasty Sethos, derives his name from this deity. But, subsequently, in the course of the Twentieth Dynasty, he is suddenly treated as an evil demon, inasmuch that his effigies and name are obliterated on all the monuments and inscriptions that could be reached." The hatred of the Osirian priests to the worship of Seth, which this conduct betokens, cannot, however, have had a sudden rise. It must have been merely the culmination of a feeling similar to that which led to the detestation in which the memory of Cheops and Cephren was held. It was, indeed, probably

* Tom. ii. p. 55.

connected with the hatred of the Pyramid builders, if we may judge from the position occupied by the god Seth. According to Bunsen, this deity was the primitive god of Northern Egypt and Palestine, and appears as the background of religious consciousness among the Semites. Moreover, his genealogy as "the Seth of Genesis, the father of Enoch (the man) must be considered as originally running parallel with that derived from the Elohim, Adam's father."* Seth, therefore, is not only the primitive god of the Semites, but also their semi-divine ancestor. We have here, probably, the explanation of a fact mentioned by Herodotus, who, after speaking of the aversion of the Egyptians for the memory of Cheops and Cephren, says, "they will not even mention their names, and for this reason they call the Pyramids after the Shepherd Philitis, who at the time of their erection used to feed his flocks near the spot." The occupation of a keeper of sheep was an abomination to the Egyptians, and if a shepherd prince dwelt near Memphis there must have been some very powerful reason for his doing so. That there was a religious reason we may infer from the

* God in History, Vol i., pp. 233-4.

stories related to Herodotus by the priests, who told him that the temples were closed during the reigns of Cheops and Cephren. M. Lenormant has, indeed, shown that this statement cannot have been correct, as an inscription preserved in the Museum at Boulak enumerates the temples built by Cheops, the pious foundations made by him, and his splendid offerings to the gods,* thus confirming the opinion expressed by Dr. Ebers. Nevertheless, there may have been some ground for the accusation of impiety made against Cheops, and it was probably his recognition of the supremacy of a god foreign to the strictly Egyptian Pantheon, which might be quite consistent with his continuing to show respect for the native gods. Who the strange deity was may probably be determined by the nationality of Philitis, whose name is mentioned in connection with the Pyramids, although they may have been erected long before his time; unless indeed the name stands for a people and not merely an individual. M. Büdenger † ingeniously identifies Philitis with Salatis, the first Hyksos king, and Prof. Duncker states that the name of the former

* Tom ii., p. 72.

† Quoted in Duncker's "History of Antiquity," Vol i. p. 98 *n.*

points to a Semitic tribe for the Hyksos, "and one immediately bordering on Egypt on the Syrian coast—the Philistines (Pelischtim), from whom the whole Syrian coast was called by the Greeks Palæstina."* The first Hyksos king fixed his residence at Memphis in the neighbourhood of the great pyramids, which had perhaps already become connected with the shepherd princes, and among a people who were probably prepared to receive him as a friend rather than as an enemy. M. Lenormant remarks that the Delta, and especially its eastern part, "appeared to have been inhabited from the highest antiquity by a population somewhat different from that of the rest of Egypt—of a more Asiatic character, and probably mixed in a certain measure with Semitic elements." That region, before even the foundation of Memphis by Menes, was for Egypt "the cradle of the worship of more important deities, who took a leading place in the national Pantheon, but in their origin were connected with the cycle of Euphratico-Syrian divinities." One of those deities was Hathor; the other was Set, "the special god of the northern country—in opposition to Horus, the god of the southern

* Duncker, Vol. i. p. 127.

country—of whose name the Soutekh of the Shepherds and of the Kheta is only an enlarged form; whom we find adored under the name of Schita in several parts of Assyria; and whom it is perhaps necessary to compare with the antediluvian patriarch Scheth (Seth) in the narrative of Genesis."* We see thus that not only was Set (Seth) by his name Soutekh the national god of the Hyksos, but he was also the chief deity of the semi-Semitic population of the Memphitic region in which that shepherd race established itself. It is not surprising, therefore, that the hatred of the native Egyptians for the Hyksos was afterwards entertained in an intensified form towards the god whom they adored, although previously, as the special deity of Lower Egypt, he had been recognised as the Agathodæmon.

The Hyksos and their congeners of Northern Egypt, however, were probably more closely connected with the ancient Cushite race, referred to by Arab tradition as the people of Ad, than with the pure Semitic stock. The Arabian branch of that race was thought to have become extinct before the establishment of the later Arabs in the peninsula. Remnants of it, however, are still

* Histoire Ancienne de l'Orient, Tom. ii. p. 147.

to be found in the territory between the Hedjaz and Yemen, and also in the Hadramaut and Mahrah, between Yemen and Oman, where a large number of independent tribes exist.* The religion of these tribes was down to a comparatively recent period star-worship, and their ancestors, the people of Ad, were adherents of the Sabaism which was so widely spread in the ancient world. To this cult the Hyksos belonged, as shown by the identification of their god Soutekh with the Seth of the Sabæans. The race connection between the population of Lower Egypt and the Hyksos, with the position occupied by Seth as the national deity, agree with the fact of Sabaism being the religion also of the northern Egyptians. Dr. Tiele, remarks that "star-worship was not unknown to the Semites, but the highly-developed astrology and magic which we find among the Babylonians and Assyrians were derived from the Akkadians," to whom the early population of Arabia, known as the people of Ad, were related. That early race, moreover, furnished the Babylonians with the

* M. Vivien de Saint-Martin, in his "Nouveau Dictionnaire de Geographie Universelle,"—art. *Arabie.* And see the "Preliminary Discourse," in Sale's "Koran," as to the tribe of Ad, and other early peoples of Arabia.

models on which their temples were built, "namely, in the form of terraced pyramids, such as were erected also in Elam, and among the oldest inhabitants of Media and India, to which class belonged the famous Tower of Babel."* The Great Pyramid of Egypt may well, therefore, have been a monument of star-worship, dedicated to the god Seth.

Nor is this conclusion, that the Great Pyramid was intimately associated with the worship of Seth, inconsistent with the fact that it appears to have been sometimes referred to by the Egyptians as the tomb of Osiris.† This opinion is connected with the myth of Osiris and Isis in its later form, which introduces Seth (Typhon) as the great enemy of Osiris. According to Bunsen, however, this form was not known earlier than the 13th or 14th century B.C., so that the Great Pyramid would not be spoken of as the tomb of Osiris before that date. It could not have been thus regarded originally, as we know that neither Cheops nor Cephren received the name of Osiris, an honour which was conferred by the Egyptian priests on the later monarch, Mycerinus, owing

* "Outlines of the History of Religion" (Eng. Trans.), p. 75.

† Dupuis, "L'Origine de tous les Cultes," Tom. I. p. 424.

to his great benevolence and justice – or, shall we say, his orthodox religious views. The learned Dupuis expresses the opinion that the Agathodæmon, or Good Spirit, whom the Sabæans believed to repose under the pyramid, was in reality Osiris, the benevolent god of Nature. The Agathodæmon of the early Egyptians was, however Seth, the special deity of Northern Egypt, and we shall not be wrong in supposing the Great Pyramid to have been erected by the Sabæans in his honour.

In so doing, we explain perfectly the scientific features which have been traced in the structure. The worshippers of the heavenly host would, undoubtedly, in so grand a religious monument as the Great Pyramid, embody all the astronomical knowledge they possessed, and this must have been considerable. The Arabian historian, Abulfaraj, as quoted by Dupuis,* says that the religion of the Chaldeans and of the Sabæans was the same, and that the former were distinguished by their astronomical observations and studied the nature of the stars and their secret influences. Nor was this true merely of the later Chaldeans. Mr. Proctor remarks, that "no one

* Tom. i. p. 7.

who considers the wonderful accuracy with which, nearly 2,000 years before the Christian era, the Chaldeans had determined the famous cycle of the Saros, can doubt that they must have observed the heavenly bodies for several centuries before they could have achieved such a success."* As to the later Chaldeans, the Jewish writer Philo observes that they make everything depend on the movement of the stars, which they regard as the sovereign arbiters of the order of the world. They limit their homage to the visible, and do not form any idea of the invisible and intellectual being; on the contrary, in observing the order of the world, they think they see in it the divinity itself, which exercises its power by the movements of the sun, the moon, the planets, and the fixed stars, by the successive revolutions of the seasons, and by the combined action of the heaven and the earth.†

A religion such as this could have no fitter monument than a vast astronomical observatory, which the Great Pyramid probably was, until at least it was completed on the death of its royal founder. The building was a worthy

* Myths and Marvels of Astronomy," p. 73.

† Treatise on Abraham, Sec. 15.

symbol of the remarkable system of religion which, according to ancient writers, once pervaded nearly the whole world, and was said to have been founded by Seth, the son of Adam. According to Philo, Abraham was educated in its principles, which he held, until having opened his eyes, he saw the light and recognised in the Universe a sovereign guide, whom he had not before suspected.

CHAPTER V

SETH AND SERPENT WORSHIP

THE association of the name of the god Seth with the Great Pyramid—a structure which appears to embody or to bear a relation to the chief scientific truths recognised by the ancient world, throws light on certain ideas entertained as to the nature of that deity. The god of intelligence of the Egyptians was Thoth, the Hermes of the Sabæans. Hermes was, however, called the son of Seth, and this deity is in some sense to be identified with Thoth. In a passage of the Book of the Dead, the former has the name Tet which, according to Bunsen, intimates that Thoth inherited many of the attributes of Seth.* It may, indeed, show that they are the same deity. Seth was the true god of Wisdom, and the pillars of Seth, on which, according to Josephus,† was inscribed the astronomical knowledge of the

* "Egypt," Vol. iii. p. 427.

† "Antiquities," Chap. ii. sec. iii.

ancient world, were the same as those mentioned in an apocryphal work ascribed to Hermes, which, according to Cedrenus, affirmed that "Enoch, foreseeing the destruction of the Earth, had inscribed the science of astronomy upon two pillars." * By these structures was probably intended the two great pyramids of Ghizeh, which appear originally to have had many inscriptions on their external coverings. Makrizi cites various authors as to the origin of the Pyramids, and among other statements it was said that that they were built by Surid, and that the First was dedicated to history and astronomy, and the Second to medical knowledge.† As Seth, Thoth, or Hermes was the god of Wisdom, so the serpent was its emblem, and especially connected with that God and with other deities of similar characteristics. "Wise as serpents‡ and harmless as doves," is an old saying, which probably has a deeper meaning than that usually ascribed to it. The connection between the serpent and the idea

* Vyse, "Operations, etc.," vol. ii. p. 330 *n.*

† Ditto, p. 354. See Appendix II. for Masoudi's account of the Legend of Surid.

‡ The Sophia, or Divine Wisdom and the Ophis-Christos of the Gnostics, was represented under the form of a serpent.—*Matter's* "Histoire Critique du Gnosticisme," Planches II. A. B. C. Matter appears to identify the Ophis with the god Kneph, p. 32.

of wisdom is well seen in the Hindu legend as to the Nagas. Mr. Fergusson remarks, "the Naga appears everywhere in Vaishnava tradition. There is no more common representation of Vishnu than as reposing on the Sesha, the celestial seven-headed snake, contemplating the creation of the world." The Upanishads refer to the science of serpents, by which is meant the wisdom of the mysterious Nagas who, according to Buddhistic legend, reside under Mount Meru, and in the waters of the terrestrial world. One of the sacred books of the Tibetan Buddhists is fabled to have been received from the Nagas, who, says Schlagentweit, are "fabulous creatures, of the nature of serpents, who occupy a place among the beings superior to man, and are regarded as protectors of the law of the Buddha. To these spiritual beings Sakyamuni is said to have taught a more philosophical religious system than to men, who were not sufficiently advanced to understand it at the time of his appearance." The serpent holds an analogous place in the religious ideas of the modern Hindus. Siva,* as Sambhu, is the patron of the Brahmanic

* Siva would seem to be the same deity as Saturn, and possibly therefore as Set (Seth), a fact which confirms the serpent character of the last named deity.

order, and, as shown by his being three-eyed, is essentially a god possessing high intellectual attributes. Vishnu also is a god of wisdom, but (notwithstanding the association with him of the Sesha), of a somewhat lower type, such as is distinctive of the worshippers of truth under its feminine aspect. The serpent has been connected with the god of Wisdom from the earliest times of which we have any historical notice. This animal was the especial symbol of Thoth or Taut, a primeval deity of Syro-Egyptian mythology, and of all those gods, such as Hermes and Seth, who can be connected with him. This is true also of the third member of the primitive Chaldean triad, Héa or Hoa. According to Sir Henry Rawlinson, the most important titles of this deity refer to "his functions as the source of all knowledge and science." Not only is he "the intelligent fish," but his name may be read as signifying both "life" and a "serpent," and he may be considered as "figured by the great serpent which occupies so conspicuous a place among the symbols of the gods on the black stones recording Babylonian benefactions." M. Lenormant identifies Héa with the fish-god Oannes of Babylonian mythology, who, according to

Berosus, "spent the whole day amongst men without taking any food, while he taught them letters, science, and the principles of every art, the rules for the foundation of towns, the building of temples, the measurement and boundaries of lands, seed-time and harvest, in short, all that could advance civilization, so that nothing new has been invented since that period."* Héa, as the god of Science, was the defender of "the frame of nature against the incessant ravages of the wicked spirits," and "help was sought from him when neither word, rite, talisman, nor even the intervention of any other of the gods had availed to destroy the demons' power."† The Chaldean god was moreover, the healer of disease,‡ in which character he resembled the God of the Hebrews, the sight of whose serpent-symbol was supposed to cure those bitten by the fiery serpents in the wilderness. There is reason to believe§ that this deity was the same as Seth, the Agathodæmon of the early Egyptians, who was represented under the form of the serpent,

* Lenormant "Chaldean Magic and Sorcery" (Eng. trans.), p. 157.

† Ditto, p. 158.

‡ Ditto, p. 21.

§ See the "Journal of Anthropology," 1870, p. 209, on this point.

and who was the giver of happiness and good fortune.* The good genius which presided over the affairs of men as the guardian spirit of their houses was a serpent, the Asp of Ranno, the snake-headed goddess who is represented as nursing the young princes. That the idea of health was among the Egyptians intimately associated with the serpent, is shown, moreover, by the crown formed of the asp, or sacred *Thermuthis*, having been given particularly to Isis, a goddess of Life and Healing. It was also the symbol of other gods of health and the like attributes, as stated by the learned Dupuis in the chapters entitled "Esculapius, Serapis, Pluto, Esmun, Cneph, and all the divinities with the attributes of the serpent"† is remarkable that a Moslem saint of Upper Egypt is still thought to appear under the form of a serpent, and to cure the diseases which afflict the pilgrims to his shrine. The power of healing is an evidence of the possession of wisdom, and so also

* Wilkinson's "Ancient Egyptians," Vol iv. p. 413. Mr. Lane states that each quarter of Cairo (which was built out of the ruins of Memphis and its tombs), is supposed to have its guardian genius or agathodæmon, in the form of a serpent.—"Manners and Customs of the Egyptians," Vol. i. p. 289.

† "Origine de tous les Cultes," Tom. ii. Part 1, p. 165.

is the power of influencing atmospheric changes. This is a most important attribute, and, as Mr. Fergusson points out, a chief characteristic of the serpents throughout the East in all ages seems to have been their power over the wind and rain. According to Colonel Meadows Taylor, in the Indian Deccan, at the present day, offerings are made to the village divinities (of whom the nag, or snake, is always one) at spring time and harvest for rain or fine weather, and also in time of cholera or other diseases or pestilence. So, among the Chinese, the dragon is regarded as the giver of rain, and in time of drought offerings are made to it. In the spring and fall, of the year it is one of the objects worshipped, by command of the Emperor, by certain mandarins. The Chinese notion of the serpent or dragon dwelling above the clouds in spring to give rain reminds us of the Aryan myth of Vritra, or Ahi, the throttling snake, or dragon with three heads, who hides away the rain-clouds, but who is slain by Indra, the beneficent giver of rain. M. Bréal says,* that "Typhon is the monster who obscures the heavens, a sort of Greek Vritra." The myth of Indra and Vritra is reproduced in

* "Mélanges de Mythologie et de Linguistique," p. 95.

Latin mythology as that of Hercules and Cacus. Cacus also is analogous to Typhon, and as the former is supposed to have taken his name from, or given it to, a certain wind which had the power of clothing itself with clouds, so the latter bore the same name as a very destructive wind which was much dreaded by the Phœnicians and Egyptians. Moreover, the name Typhon was given by the Egyptians to anything tempestuous and hence to the Ocean.

We have here a reference to the serpent as the embodiment of the Evil Being; and in the later identification of Seth with Typhon, the enemy of Osiris, we have evidence of the connection of the serpent with the former deity. M. Lenormant tells us that, "evil was personified in a particular god, Set or Soutekh,* called also sometimes Baal, who was the supreme god of the neighbouring Asiatic populations, and, at a later period, of the shepherd kings; the Greeks considered him the same as their Typhon, and it was said that Osiris hadsuccumbed to his blows."†

* The earlier character of this deity is well shown by the remark of Tiele, that the name Sutech is an attempt to reproduce in Egyptian form the Semitic divine name, Sedeq, "the righteous." —"Outlines of the History of Religion," p. 55.

† "Chaldean Magic," p. 83.

The name Typhon appears to have been given more especially to the Evil Being, as the opponent of Horus, who was, however, the same deity as Osiris, whose son he was said to be. The former was then represented as Apap or Apophis, or the giant serpent, who was pierced by the spear of Horus, as the serpent Pytho was slain by Apollo.* Henceforth Seth, instead of being regarded by the Egyptians as the Agathodæmon, was looked upon as the principle of evil. The same change took place among the Accadian population of Media. M. Lenormant states that the "worship of serpent-gods is found amongst many of the Turanian tribes. The Accadians made the serpent one of the principal attributes, and one of the forms of Héa." When once, however, "the Iranian traditions were fused with the ancient beliefs of the Proto-Medic religion, the serpent-god naturally became identified with the representative of the dark and bad principle, for, according to the Mazdean myths, the serpent was the form assumed by

* "Chaldean Magic," p. 83; Wilkinson, Vol. iv. pp. 395, 435—Apophis, may have given name to Papi, and Egyptian king, who lived about a century after Cheops, and also to Apepi, or Apappos one of the Hyksos kings, unless the 'Giant' Serpent took this title from the former monarch.

Angromainyus, in order to penetrate into the heaven of Ahuramazda."* Here is the conflict between light and darkness, and between life and death, which is reproduced in Egyptian mythology, where the evil principle is represented in the one case by the serpent Apap, and in the other by Set † (Seth), whose symbol was the serpent.

The association between the serpent and the idea of darkness had an astronomical foundation. The position which the constellation Draco at one time occupied showed that the Great Serpent was the ruler of the night. This constellation was formerly at the very centre of the heavens, and it is so extensive, that it was called the Great Dragon. Its body spreads over seven signs of the Zodiac, and Dupuis, who sees in the Dragon of the Apocalypse a reference to the celestial serpent, says, "It is not astonishing that a constellation so extended should be represented by the author of that book as a great dragon with seven heads, who drew the third part of the stars from heaven and cast them to the earth." ‡

* "Chaldean Magic," p. 232.

† Tiele, "Outlines of the History of Religions," p. 47; also, "History of the Egyptian Religion," Vol. i. p. 72.

‡ Dupuis, Tom. iii. p. 255.

Moreover, when the constellation Draco occupied its elevated position, it supplied the pole-star of the heavens. The importance of this fact, in connection with the erection of the Great Pyramid, will be understood after what has been said as to the association of the Pyramid with the god Seth. That structure was erected, not only as a tomb for its founder, but as a monumental temple in honour of a deity whose special symbol was the serpent, the emblem of wisdom with the primitive race whose religion would appear to have been a combination of serpent-worship and Sabaism. The Great Pyramid is thus a monument not only of Sabaism, but of serpent-worship, and, as such, its scientific as well as its astronomical character receives the proper explanation. The builders of such a temple would apply their utmost skill in its construction and they would seek to preserve in it, as far as possible, the scientific knowledge which they had derived from their ancestors.

According to a Coptic MS., upon the walls of the Pyramids were written the mysteries of science, astronomy, geometry, physic, and much useful knowledge. The same MS. states, that they were built before the Flood by Surid, for safety, and as tombs for himself and household.* It is remarkable that, as Sir Gardner Wilkinson points out, Tuphán, which appears to be the same word as Typhon, the name of the Evil Being, is the Arabic name of the Deluge.† The association of the Pyramids with a flood has, however, a purely astronomical explanation. Mr. Proctor, when speaking of the position of the pole-star Alpha Draconis, at the date of the erection of the Great Pyramid, says,‡ "We know that in the past the constellation of the Dragon was at the pole, or boss, of the celestial sphere. In stellar temples, like those of which Rawlinson gives examples, the Dragon would be the uppermost or ruling constellation. And here, in passing, it may interest the reader to note that, some find evidence in this relation that when writers of old spoke of the Old Dragon as having been cast from heaven, carrying two-thirds of the celestial beings with him, reference was made —unconsciously, perhaps, on the narrator's part

* Vyse, "Operations," etc., Vol. ii. p. 330, and see Appendix II.

† "The Ancient Egyptians," Vol. iv. p. 427 *n.*

‡ *Knowledge*, Vol. i. p. 243.

—to some tradition of the passing away or fall of the Dragon from its former ruling position among the constellations. Those who thus interpret ancient records (much more ancient than Jewish history), find in Hercules, with his heel assailed by the serpent, as in our constellation figures, the first Adam; in Ophinchus, the serpent holder, the second Adam. In Argo they find the Ark—in fact, in a whole series of constellations they find the story of the Flood. In Aquarius, with the streams pouring from his water-jug, they find the beginning of the Flood. In the river Eridanus and the seas in which Pisces and the great sea-monster Cetus seem to swim, they see pictured the prevalence of deep water over the whole earth. The Raven of the Heavens is the raven of the Flood-narrative. Argo is the Ark, shown as if only the stern-half of a great ship lodged in the mountain. The Centaur, bearing sacrifice, as Aratus says, to Ara, the altar, is Noah offering sacrifice after he had left the Ark; and the bow of Sagittarius in the smoke (the Milky-way), which seems to ascend from the altar, is the bow of promise. These may, of course, be only fancies, but it is singular how closely these constellations, which are among the few really seeming to picture recognisable objects in the heavens, correspond in sequence and in range of right ascension with the events recorded respecting the Flood." *

Fancies or not, it is unquestionable that the Deluge has been associated in the legends of some Eastern peoples, not only with the Pyramids,† but also with the constellations. Thus it is with the Chaldean legend, according to which Saturn in a dream announced the coming catastrophe to Xixutrus, who, like Noah, escaped in an ark. The Assyrian tablets discovered by the late Dr. Smith, and which contain what is called the Nimrod Epic, have preserved a similar account of the Deluge. It is now established that the twelve cantos of that Epic "refer to the annual course of the sun through the twelve months of the year. Each tablet answers to a special month, and contains a distinct reference to the animal forms in the signs of the Zodiac." Thus, "the Deluge forms the subject of the eleventh canto, corresponding

* *Knowledge*, Vol. i. p. 243 — Dupuis explains fully the position of the heavens at the date of what he terms the "sacred fiction" of the Deluge, Tom. iii. p. 176, *seq.*

† See Appendix II. for the Arabian legend as to the connection between the Deluge and the building of the Pyramids.

with the month of Skebat (Feb.—Jan.), which is consecrated to Rimmon, the god of storms and rain, and harmonises with the eleventh sign of the Zodiac—Aquarius, or the Waterman. The latter month is styled in Sumerish-Accadian 'the month of the curse of the rain,' or, as we might almost say, the Deluge month."* The ancient Babylonians are usually accredited with the invention of the worship of the heavenly bodies, and the existence among them of the deluge myth in connection with the constellations is an important fact. It is no less important in relation to the question of the object of the Great Pyramid, that the capital of Babylonia contained a structure described by Strabo as a pyramid dedicated to the worship of the planetary bodies, exceeding in size the great Egyptian monument itself, and much resembling the Egyptian Pyramid of Degrees at Sakkarah. The Babylonian Tower was at the base a square of 600 feet, and consisted of eight towers, each 75 feet high, one above the other, making a total height of 600 feet. M. Lenormant speaks of the erection of this temple as having been attri-

* "The Nineteenth Century," 1882, p. 236.

buted to "the most ancient king, the first king," and he says it was "the tangible expression, the material and architectural manifestation, of the Chaldaic-Babylonian religion. Serving both as a sanctuary and as an observatory for the stars, it agreed admirably with the genius of the essentially siderial religion to which it was united by an indissoluble bond"*—language which might be used with exactly the same propriety of the Great Pyramid itself.

That the erection of the Great Pyramid had some connection with the constellations is not at all improbable. We have already seen that Mr. Proctor prefers the date 3350 B.C. to the later one of 2170 B.C. for the building of the pyramid. The latter date would seem, however, to be the more probable one. That it was erected during the reign of Cheops† is almost universally admitted; and, although the time when he reigned has not been satisfactorily established, there are grounds for believing it to have been about 2200 B.C. Prof. C. Piazzi Smyth affirms that

* "Chaldean Magic," p. 322.

† If Soris was the first monarch of the Fourth Dynasty, the Great Pyramid may possibly have been commenced in his reign, and completed during that of Cheops.

"the only monumental conclusion formed by comparing the quarry marks of the Great Pyramid with whatever is to be trusted, or is tolerably agreed upon among Egyptologists, and both of them with an astronomical date of the buildings,—can be no other than that two of the kings of the Fourth Dynasty of Egyptian history —Shofo and Nu-Shofo by name—lived through a period including the epoch of 2170 B.C."* It is true that, as Prof. Smyth points out, this date differs from that fixed by nearly all modern Egyptologists,† although it agrees very nearly with the date 2228 B.C., assigned for the commencement of the Fourth Dynasty by Mr. Wm. Osburn, the author of the "Monumental History of Egypt." It is consistent, moreover, with the chronological facts given by Dr. Birch. This Egyptologist gives 3000 B.C. for the commencement of the first dynasty; and if this Dynasty continued for 263 years, the Second Dynasty for 306 years, and the Third Dynasty for 214 years, as stated by Manetho, we have 2223 B.C. as the date of

* "Life and Work at the Great Pyramid," Vol. iii. p. 338.

† M. Vivien de Saint-Martin gives 3893 B.C. as the best date for the epoch of Menes.—"Nouveau Dict. de Geographie Universelle," Art. *Egypte*.

the commencement of the Fourth Dynasty, and therefore of the erection of the Great Pyramid, if Cheops was its builder. Curiously enough, however, this is about the date fixed for the origin of the constellations. Mr. Proctor states that between 2100 and 2200 years before the Christian era the southern constellations had their original position, the invisible southern pole then lying at the centre of the space free from constellations. He adds, " It is noteworthy that for other reasons this period, or rather a definite epoch within it, is indicated as that to which must be referred the beginning of exact astronomy. Amongst others must be mentioned this—that in the year 2170 B.C. *quam proxime*, the Pleiades rose to their highest above the horizon at noon (or technically made their noon culmination) at the spring equinox. We can readily understand that to minds possessed with full faith in the influence of the stars on the earth, this fact would have great significance." At that epoch the southernmost constellations would be seen in their natural position—standing upright when above the southern horizon at midnight. On those grounds, Mr. Proctor affirms that the period when the old southern constellations were formed must have been between 2400 and 2000 years before the Christian era. He deems it highly probable, moreover, that the year 2170 B.C. may be regarded as the date, not of the beginning of astronomy, but of the introduction of a new astronomical system, the substitution of the use of the twelve zodiacal signs for that of the twenty-eight lunar mansions. Assuming that conclusion to be correct, we have a most remarkable coincidence between the date of the invention of the Zodiac and that of the erection of the Great Pyramid. If it is true, however, as Dupuis supposed, that the Egyptians invented the constellations, the agreement between those dates was probably more than a coincidence. The French writer remarks, "The figures traced in the Zodiac and in the other constellations have not been placed there haphazard: they are the hieroglyphic calendar of the ancient peoples; they are connected with their wants and their climate; and they all have a meaning in their origin, although it may be difficult for us now to discover the sense of all the symbols." Dupuis shows what was the primitive position of the constellations, considered as the astronomical and rural calendar of a people both intellectual and agricultural, and he affirms that it accords perfectly with the agriculture of Egypt, and at the same time with the position of the solstitial and equinoctial points in the heavens at a certain epoch. Moreover, owing to the difference in the order of agricultural operations followed in Egypt from that in other climates, the rural calendar which fitted the Egyptians could not suit any other people, and therefore he ascribes to them the honour of having invented the astronomical sciences; a conclusion supported, it is said, by the fact that the Egyptians regarded their Zodiac, not only as a rural and meteorological calendar, but as the base of all their religion and of their astronomy.* M. Flammarion appears to doubt whether Dupuis has satisfactorily established his theory of the origin of the constellations,† and the date fixed by Mr. Proctor for the formation of the Zodiac is hardly consistent with that theory. It is possible, however, that whilst the constellations were formed by the Chaldeans long before that date, the zodiacal signs were only then arranged

* "Origine de tous les Cultes," Tom. iii. p. 339.

† "Histoire du Ciel," p. 153.

in an order to accord with the climate of Egypt by settlers in this country. Mr. Proctor, after fixing the probable limits of the place where the constellations were formed, at from 35 to 39 degrees north of the equator, says, "The Great Pyramid, as we know, is about 30 degrees north of the Equator; but we also know that its architects travelled southwards to find a suitable place for it. One of their objects may have been to obtain a fuller view of the star-sphere south of their constellations."* This suggestion is a very important one, for it assumes that the constellations were formed before the erection of the Pyramid, and therefore that the date of the latter event cannot have been earlier than that of the former. Mr. Proctor goes further, however, and even suggests that one of the objects which the architects of the Great Pyramid may have had was "the erection of a building indicating the epoch when the new system was entered upon, and defining in its proportions, its interior passages, and other features, fundamental elements of the new system." The construction of that building implies considerable proficiency in astronomical observation,

* "Myths," etc., p. 362.

and hence, says Mr. Proctor, "the year 2170 B.C. may very well be regarded as defining the introduction of a new system of astronomy, but certainly not the beginning of astronomy itself.*" That year becomes, however, the date of the pyramid itself, and in the suggestion that it was intended to commemorate the substitution of the twelve zodiacal signs for the twenty-eight lunar mansions, we have a strong confirmation of the opinion expressed in these pages that the Great Pyramid was a monument of Sabaism, and that it was erected in honour of Seth, the Agathodæmon of the ancient world, and consecrated to his worship.

* Ditto, p. 360.

NOTE

ONE of the most curious series of relations found by the Pyramidists is connected with the Great Coffer, or sarcophagus, of the King's Chamber. John Taylor and his followers assert that this coffer is the same in capacity with the Ark and with the Laver of the Hebrew Tabernacle, and that the Molten Sea of Solomon's Temple was just fifty times such capacity, and exactly equal in interior cubic space with the contents of the King's Chamber itself. There is nothing absurd or improbable in there being some such relation between those vessels, if the Pyramid was a temple dedicated to the god Seth. Judging, indeed, from the analogy presented by Hindoo usage, the coffer was "a sacred trough, filled by the Priests on certain festivals with sacramental water and lotus-flowers." This explanation of its use was given to Mr. St. John by some learned Brahmins, who said that the

Great Pyramid was a temple, and that if it had an underground communication with the Nile it must have been intended for the worship of Pad Madévi.* An early English writer, Mr. Shaw, would seem to have been much of the same opinion, as he thought the coffer was intended for the celebration of the mystical worship of Osiris, and he supposed it to have contained images, sacred vestments and utensils, or water for lustration. If for Osiris we substitute Seth that opinion will be near the truth. The so-called King's Chamber, of which an enthusiastic pyramidist says, "The polished walls, fine materials, grand proportions, and exalted place eloquently tell of glories yet to come," if not "the chamber of perfections"† of Cheops's tomb, was probably the place to which the initiant was admitted after he had passed through the narrow upward passage and the grand gallery, with its lowly termination, which gradually prepared him for the final stage of the sacred mysteries.

* Referred to by Col. Vyse, "Operations," etc., Vol ii. p. 313.

† This was one of the names of the principal chamber of a tomb. See "Records of the Past," Vol xii. Egyptian Texts, p. 106.

APPENDIX I

The following is Dr. Sprenger's account (taken from Arab and Syrian sources) of Seth and Hermes, in connection with the Pyramids of Ghizeh. He says (as quoted by Col. Vyse in the 2nd vol. of his work, p. 364):—

"In Abul Feda's 'Historia Anteislamitica,' edited by Fleisher, p. 16, it is stated, that Syria was one of the earliest inhabited countries, and that the Syriac language was the first that was spoken; that the Sabæan language was established by Seth and Edris (Enoch); that there was a town called Haran, to which pilgrims resorted, as they did to the two large Pyramids of Ghizeh, one of which was said to be the tomb of Edris, and the other of his son Syabi; where they celebrated as a festival the day on which the sun entered the sign of Aries. In the 'Melelwa Nahil,' MS., 47 in Nic. Cat., Hermes is represented as the pupil of Agathodæmon. In another account, MS. 785, Uri's Cat. Agathodæmon is mentioned as a King of Egypt. The Sabæans consider the Great Pyramid of Ghizeh as the tomb of Seth; the Second, that of Hermes; and the Third, that of Izabi; while the Copts state that the Great Pyramid is the tomb of Surid; the Second, that of Herjib, or Haukith, his brother; the Third, that of his son."

Dr. Sprenger says, further:—"In the Syrian chronicle of Bar-Hebræus (translated into Latin by Professor Bruns), Enoch is said to have invented letters and architecture, under the title of Trismigistus, or of Hermes, to have built many cities and established laws, to have taught the worship of God,* and astronomy, to give alms and tithes, to offer up first fruits, libations, etc., to abstain from unlawful foods, and drunkenness, and to keep feasts at the rising of the sun, or new moons, and at the ascent of the planets. His pupil was Agathodæmon (Seth); according to other accounts, Asclepiades, a king renowned for wisdom, who, when Enoch was translated, set up an image in honour of him, and thereby introduced idolatry. The Egyptians are supposed to have been descended from these persons.

* This agrees with the Biblical statement that in the days of Enos men began "to call on the name of the Lord," Gen. iv. 26.

According to Hadgi Walfah, they derived their knowledge from the Chaldeans, who are said to have been the Persian Magi, and to have originally come from Babylon. The statues of the Grecian Hermes, which seem to agree in name with the Pyramids (Haram), were not images, but symbols of the deity and of the generative principle of nature in the form of obelisks (see Winkelman, Book i., Cap. i. 1011.) Statues of this kind sacred to Hermes were erected by the Greeks in honour of distinguished heroes; and the same allegorical allusion might have been kept in view when the Pyramids were constructed as tombs. The Egyptian account, however, of Hermes, is very obscure; that person is mentioned in the 'Burham-i-Kati' as the son of Rahman, son of Isfendiar, and to have arrived from the East. One of the sons of Aunshirwan has also that title. Hormig is the name of the first day of the month, which is considered propitious for any undertaking; and it is a name of the planet Mercury; and Wednesday (dies Mercurii) was sacred to him: for to most of the planets days were attributed, in which their influence was supposed to govern human affairs, and even Mohammedan superstition assigned to children born on these days various qualities, characteristic of the heathen personifications of the different planets. Hermes is mentioned in many astrological treatises as presiding over the sixth climate. An idea, a period of time, or any remarkable occurrence, were frequently connected with ideal persons in mythology, and when any similarity existed received the same appellation. In this manner there were five Hermes; and the fifth was the Oriental Hermes who was worshipped by the Phineatæ, and is said to have fled after the death of Argus into Egypt, and to have civilized that country under the name of Thoth. This coincides with the account of Tifashi, which is evidently taken from an Egyptian tradition; reference may also be made to Plato, Philel. 21, 24, Phædro, p. 340. Hermes was likewise distinguished by his wisdom; and was reported to have been buried in a great building called Abou Hermes, which, together with another, the tomb of his wife, or of his son, was afterwards named Haraman. These were the two large Pyramids, and the form of their construction was called Makhrut."

APPENDIX II

MASOUDI, who died in the year 967 A.D., professes to relate the Coptic tradition, which says, "that Surid* Ben Shaluk Ben Sermuni Ben Termidun Ben Tedresan Ben Sal, one of the kings of Egypt before the Flood, built the two great pyramids; and notwithstanding they were subsequently named after a person called Sheddad Ben Ad, that they were not built by the Adites, who could not conquer Egypt, on account of the powers which the Egyptians possessed by means of enchantment; that the reason for

* Surid may be the same as Suphis or Cheops, as in a papyrus said to have been found in the monastery of Abou-Hormeis, Surid is said to have been buried in the eastern (Great) Pyramid, his brother Haukith in the western, and his nephew Karwars in the smaller pyramid. (Vyse, "Operations," etc., vol. ii. p. 332.)—Surid appears to be given in the list of Manetho, under the name of Sôris, as the first king of the fourth dynasty. This king is, however, treated by M. Lenormant as non-historical. (*See* List of the Kings of Egypt, "Histoire Ancienne de l'Orient," tom. ii. p. 430), and he refers to Khoufou (Suphis) the tablet at the mouth of the ancient mine at Sinai, which English Egyptologists ascribe to Soris (Shuré). The name of this king is also said to have been found in the tombs near Ghizeh, and in the quarry marks of the northern pyramid of Abou-Seir, which is, therefore, thought to be his tomb. (Sir J. G. Wilkinson, in Rawlinson's "Herodotus," vol. ii. p. 344, 346).

building the Pyramids was the following dream, which happened to Surid three hundred years previous to the Flood. It appeared to him, that the earth was overthrown, and that the inhabitants were laid prostrate upon it; that the stars wandered confusedly from their courses, and clashed together with a tremendous noise. The king, although greatly affected by this vision, did not disclose it to any person, but was conscious that some great event was about to take place." Soon afterwards the king had another vision, which so much alarmed him that he repaired to the Temple of the Sun, "where, with great lamentations, he prostrated himself in the dust. Early in the morning he assembled the chief priests from all the Nomes of Egypt, a hundred and thirty in number. No other persons were admitted to this assembly, when he related his first and his second vision. The interpretation was declared to announce, 'that some great event would take place.'" The high-priest, whose name was Philimon, or Iklimon, related a dream which he had had a year before, in which the firmament descended till it overshadowed him and the king like a vault as they sat upon the tower of Amasis. "The king then directed the astrologers to ascertain, by taking the altitude, whether the stars foretold any great catastrophe, and the result announced an approaching deluge.* The king ordered them to inquire, whether or not this calamity would befal Egypt; and they answered, Yes, the flood will overwhelm the land, and destroy a large portion of it for some years. He ordered them to inquire if the earth would again become fruitful, or if it would continue to be covered with water. They answered that its former fertility would return. The king demanded what would then happen. He was informed that a stranger would invade the country, kill the inhabitants, and seize upon their property; and that afterwards a deformed people, coming from beyond the Nile, would take possession of the kingdom, upon which the king ordered the Pyramids to be built, and the predictions of the priests to be inscribed upon columns, and upon the large stones belonging to them; and he placed within them his treasures, and all his valuable property, together with the bodies of his ancestors. He also ordered the priests to deposit within them written accounts of their wisdom and acquirements in the different arts

* According to Makrizi, fire was to proceed from the sign Leo, and to consume the world.

and sciences.* Subterraneous channels were also constructed to convey to them the waters of the Nile. He filled the passages with talismans, with wonderful things and idols, and with the writings of the priests, containing all manner of wisdom, the names and properties of medical plants, and the sciences of arithmetic and geometry, that they might remain as records, for the benefit of those who would afterwards comprehend them." After describing the construction of the three pyramids, Masoudi, says, "In the eastern (Great) Pyramid were inscribed the heavenly spheres, and figures representing the stars and planets in the forms in which they were worshipped. The king also deposited the instruments and the thuribula with which his forefathers had sacrificed to the stars, and also their writings; likewise, the position of the stars and their circles, together with the history and chronicles of time past, of that which is to come, and of every future event which would take place in Egypt. He placed there, also, coloured basins (for lustration and sacrificial purposes),

* Masoudi says that all these marvellous things were placed within the Pyramids; whilst Makrizi, on the authority of Usted Ibrahim, particularises the subterraneous passages as the depositories. On the margin of one of Makrizi's MSS., we read that the inscriptions of the priests were on the ceilings, roofs, etc., of the subterraneous passages.

with pure water, and other matters." After referring to the deposit of the bodies of the priests in the coloured (Third) Pyramid, Masoudi describes the guardians assigned by the king to each pyramid. "The guardian of the eastern pyramid was an idol of speckled granite, standing upright, with a weapon like a spear in his hand; a serpent was wreathed round his head, which seized upon and strangled whoever approached, by twisting round his neck, when it again returned to its former position upon the idol. . . . When everything was finished, he caused the Pyramids to be haunted with living spirits; and offered up sacrifices to prevent the intrusion of strangers, and of all persons excepting those who by their conduct were wor hy of admission." The author then says, that, according to the Coptic account, the following passage was inscribed, in Arabic, upon the Pyramids: "I, Surid the King, have built these Pyramids, and have finished them in sixty-one years. Let him, who comes after me, and imagines himself a king like me, attempt to destroy them in six hundred. To destroy is easier than to build. I have clothed them with silk: let him try to cover them with mats."*

* Col. Vyse, "Operations," etc., Vol. ii. p. 322 *seq.*

What follows are Appendix notes to one of Wake's primary sources for this book—*Operations at the Pyramids of Gizah* by Col. Richard Howard-Vyse. This information comes from Volume 2 of the 3 volume set, now extremely rare, first published in London in 1840. Several vital manuscripts are covered here from the British Museum. This includes Masoudi's, which has since deteriorated, but its knowledge is preserved here through the words of Dr. Sprenger who studied it closely, among others referenced. The original source for these fragments comes from ancient traditions, either passed down verbally through the Coptics or preserved somehow from the Library at Alexandria, that burned down centuries ago.

MASOUDI,[5]

DIED 345 A.H.

THE manuscript of the Akbar Ezzeman, at Oxford, was so much decayed, that recourse has been had to the works of other authors, who have given the same account in nearly the same words— namely, to Makrizi, who quotes from Usted Ibrahim Ben

[5] M. Jomard concludes from this author, that the Pyramids were covered with continuous inscriptions, written by nations long since perished; and he appears to consider that this account is correct, particularly as it is corroborated by Ebn Haukal, and likewise by William De Baldensel,* who lived in the fourteenth century, and said, that he saw inscriptions in various characters upon the two larger Pyramids. It is to be remarked, however, that this only proves that some part of them had been written upon; and other authors have mentioned Latin verses, &c., that had been inscribed in the same manner as the names of travellers, which are now to be seen upon the top of the Great Pyramid. M. Jomard then states, upon the authority of Dionysius Telmahre, that the Pyramids were solid buildings, erected over the tombs of antient kings; and from the same author, that the height of the Pyramids was two hundred and fifty cubits, and that their bases were squares of five hundred cubits; and also that he had examined an excavation fifty cubits deep, which had been made in one of them, and found that it had been built of hewn stones, from five to ten cubits in length.

* M. Jomard seems to have taken this account from M. De Sacy.

Wasyff Shah; to Soyuti; to a MS. (No. 7503) in the British Museum, entitled "The Odour of Flowers," or "the Wonders of Different Countries, by Mohammed Ben Ayas;" to a Turkish "History of Egypt," MS. (7861) in British Museum, written 1089, A.H.; and to Yakut, MS. in the Bodleian Library.

Masoudi's account professes to relate the Coptic tradition, which says, "That Surid, Ben Shaluk, Ben Sermuni, Ben Termidun, Ben Tedresan, Ben Sal, one of the kings of Egypt before the flood, built the two great Pyramids; and, notwithstanding they were subsequently named after a person called Sheddad Ben Ad, that they were not built by the Adites, who could not conquer Egypt, on account of the powers, which the Egyptians possessed by means of enchantment; that the reason for building the Pyramids was the following dream, which happened to Surid three hundred years previous to the flood. It appeared to him, that the earth was overthrown, and that the inhabitants were laid prostrate upon it; that the stars wandered confusedly from their courses, and clashed together with a tremendous noise. The king, although greatly affected by this vision, did not disclose it to any person, but was conscious that some great event was about to take place. Soon afterwards in another vision, he saw the fixed stars descend upon the earth in the form of white birds, and seizing the people, enclose them in a cleft between two great mountains, which shut upon them. The stars were dark, and veiled with smoke. The king awoke in great consternation, and repaired to the temple of the sun, where, with great lamentations, he prostrated himself in the dust. Early in the morning he assembled the chief priests from all the nomes of Egypt, a hundred and thirty in number; no other persons were admitted to this assembly, when he related his first and second vision. The interpretation was declared to announce, "that some great event would take place."

The high priest, whose name was Philimon or Iklimon, spoke as follows:—"Grand and mysterious are thy dreams: The visions of the king will not prove deceptive, for sacred is his majesty.[6] I

[6] These words and the designation of the high-priests, and the general tenour of the story are not Arabic. The king is represented as being of a superior order, and the sacred organ of the priests; but the caliphs, and even Mahomet, however greatly reverenced by Mahometans, are always considered mere human beings; and although the caliphs were invested with supreme authority, their viziers and councils confined their deliberations to politics, and did not interfere with religious affairs.—*Dr. Sprenger.*

will now declare unto the king a dream, which I also had a year ago, but which I have not imparted to any human being." The king said, "Relate it, O Philimon."[7] The high-priest accordingly began: — "I was sitting with the king upon the tower of Amasis. The firmament descended from above till it overshadowed us like a vault. The king raised his hands in supplication to the heavenly bodies, whose brightness was obscured in a mysterious and threatening manner. The people ran to the palace to implore the king's protection; who in great alarm again raised his hands towards the heavens, and ordered me to do the same; and behold, a bright opening appeared over the king, and the sun shone forth above; these circumstances allayed our apprehensions, and indicated, that the sky would resume its former altitude; and fear together with the dream vanished away."[8]

The king then directed the astrologers to ascertain by taking the altitude whether the stars foretold any great catastrophe, and the result announced an approaching deluge.[9] The king ordered them to inquire whether or not this calamity would befal Egypt; and they answered, yes, the flood will overwhelm the land, and destroy a large portion of it for some years.[1]

[7] Some histories say that Philimon was with Noah in the ark.—*Dr. Sprenger.*

[8] The above-mentioned MS. 7503, on the authority of Usted Ibrahim Ben Wasyff Shah, relates another vision of the high-priest, as follows·—"I saw the town of Amasis, together with its inhabitants, overthrown. The images of the gods (idols) cast down from their places, and personages coming down from Heaven, and smiting with iron maces the inhabitants of the earth. I asked them why they did so? They answered, Because these people did not believe in their gods. I asked if there were means of security? They answered, Yes, whoever seeks will find it from the Master of the Ark (Noah). I was overcome with alarm" It is remarkable, that Makrizi in this passage, "They do not believe on their gods," writes their gods, and not their idols, which latter words he uses in all other instances, in accordance with the Mahometan custom of mentioning with contempt heathen deities. Soyuti renders this passage, "they do not believe on Bramah, who created them." The word Kafar is accompanied with a substantive in an accusative case, when it signifies "to disbelieve in." The B, therefore, in the word Barahm, is not to be considered a preposition, but part of the word, which is Barahm Brahma, and not Rahm, or Rama.—*Dr. Sprenger.*

[9] According to Makrizi, fire was to proceed from the sign Leo, and to consume the world. A further continuation of this story is also given, on the authority of Ustad Ibrahim, whose detail was derived from a papyrus found in the monastery of Abou Hormeis, a document, which will be afterwards alluded to.—*Dr. Sprenger.*

[1] Besides the general deluge mentioned in holy writ, Dr. Sprenger is of opinion, that a partial inundation took place in Egypt, and on the shores of the Mediter-

He ordered them to inquire if the earth would again become fruitful, or if it would continue to be covered with water. They answered that its former fertility would return. The king demanded what would then happen. He was informed that a stranger would invade the country, kill the inhabitants, and seize upon their property; and that afterwards a deformed people, coming from beyond the Nile, would take possession of the kingdom;[2] upon which the king ordered the Pyramids to be built, and the predictions of the priests to be inscribed upon columns, and upon the large stones belonging to them; and he placed within them his treasures, and all his valuable property, together with the bodies of his ancestors. He also ordered the priests to deposit within them, written accounts of their wisdom and acquirements in the different arts and sciences.[3] Subter-

ranean Sea, described by Masoudi, and alluded to by Abul Feda; whether the supposition be true or not, it is extremely probable, that after the great and miraculous event, large bodies of water were left on the higher levels, which from time to time may have been increased by the melting of snow and by other natural causes, till, bursting through their respective barriers they produced, without the special intervention of Almighty power, at different times, partial inundations, and other alterations in the surface of the earth, which, under Divine Providence, may have had the salutary effect of keeping in human remembrance the former tremendous judgment. The destruction of the earth by fire and water, (both which agents may be supposed to have been co-existent, since without water no volcanic effects can be produced), and the idea of a resuscitation of the world after a certain period, appear to have been alluded to by the Hindoos in their mythology, and also by the Parsees; and Herodotus states, that this was also the belief of the antient Egyptians, and terms it ἐκπύρωσις. It would be perhaps difficult to ascertain whether these ideas proceeded from traditions of the universal deluge, or of the final consummation of the globe. The learned doctor then repeats his opinion, that the fable of Surid having built the Pyramids before the deluge, is not of Arabic origin, but that it is possible that they were erected with the vain idea of providing against the recurrence of a similar event; and that the tower of Babel, built for somewhat the like purpose, may have been a Pyramid. He concludes, with great probability, that these monuments were constructed by people of the same nation, who, he conjectures, established the religious institutions at Babylon, came to Egypt from Iran, and were termed by the Arabs, Edris (teachers); by the Egyptians, Tauth; and by the Greeks and Persians, Hermes; and, as a term of hostility, Cushites.

[2] These deformed people appear to be the men of ignoble birth, out of the eastern parts, mentioned by Manetho.

[3] Masoudi says that all these marvellous things were placed within the Pyramids, whilst Makrizi, on the authority of Usted Ibrahim, particularises the subterraneous passages as the depositories. On the margin of one of Makrizi's MSS., we read that the inscriptions of the priests were on the ceilings, roofs, &c., of the subterraneous passages.—*Dr. Sprenger.*

raneous channels were also constructed to convey to them the waters of the Nile.[4] He filled the passages[5] with talismans, with wonderful things, and idols; and with the writings of the priests, containing all manner of wisdom, the names and properties of medical plants, and the sciences of arithmetic and of geometry; that they might remain as records, for the benefit of those, who could afterwards comprehend them.

He ordered pillars to be cut, and an extensive pavement to be formed. The lead employed in the work was procured from the West. The stone came from the neighbourhood of Es Souan. In this way were built the Three Pyramids at Dashoor,[6] the eastern, western, and the coloured one. In carrying on the work, leaves of papyrus, or paper, inscribed with certain characters, were placed under the stones prepared in the quarries; and upon being struck, the blocks were moved at each time the distance of a bowshot (about one hundred and fifty cubits), and so by degrees arrived at the Pyramids.[7] Rods of iron were inserted into the centres of the stones, that formed the pavement, and, passing through the blocks placed upon them, were fixed by melted lead. Entrances, with porticoes composed of stones fastened together with lead, were made forty cubits under the earth: the length of every portico being one hundred and fifty cubits. The door of the eastern Pyramid was one hundred cubits eastward from the centre of the face, in which it was placed, and was in the building itself. The door of the western Pyramid was one hundred cubits westward, and was also in the building. And the door of the coloured Pyramid was one hundred cubits southward of the centre, and

[4] يدخل فيها النيل الي مكان بعينه These are the words of the original; they are not clear, and may mean the channel for the whole stream, which was, according to Makrizi and Soyuti (but not to Masoudi), constructed for the conveyance of the water into Upper Egypt, and to the westward, in which case, it is to be observed, the water must have flowed up hill.—*Dr. Sprenger.*

[5] It is stated, apparently on the authority of Usted Ibrahim, that these passages are forty cubits under the earth; and that the foundations of the Pyramids were afterwards laid at four hundred royal cubits, or, according to some, five hundred, each of which is equal to two common cubits; and that the base was a space of one hundred cubits.—*Dr. Sprenger.*

[6] Makrizi and Soyuti do not mention Dashoor, so that the author probably alluded to the Pyramids of Gizeh, as Dashoor is only inserted in a MS. in the Bodleian.—*Dr. Sprenger.*

[7] This may be a symbolical manner of expressing that they moved the large stones by mechanical powers which were described upon books or leaves, or it may allude to the quarry-marks.

was likewise in the building. The height of each Pyramid was one hundred royal cubits, equal to five hundred common cubits. The squares of the bases were the same. They were began at the eastern side. When the buildings were finished, the people assembled with rejoicing around the king, who covered the Pyramids with coloured brocade, from the top to the bottom, and gave a great feast, at which all the inhabitants of the country were present.

He constructed, likewise, with coloured granite, in the western Pyramid, thirty repositories for sacred symbols, and talismans formed of sapphires, for instruments of war composed of iron, which could not become rusty, and for glass, which could be bent without being broken; and also for many sorts of medicines, simple and compound, and for deadly poisons.

In the eastern Pyramid were inscribed the heavenly spheres, and figures representing the stars and planets in the forms, in which they were worshipped.[8]

The king, also, deposited the instruments, and the thuribula, with which his forefathers had sacrificed to the stars, and also their writings; likewise, the positions of the stars, and their circles; together with the history and chronicles of time past, of that, which is to come, and of every future event, which would take place in Egypt. He placed there, also, coloured basins (for lustration and sacrificial purposes), with pure water, and other matters.[9]

Within the coloured Pyramid were laid the bodies of the deceased priests, in sarcophagi of black granite; and with each was a book, in which the mysteries of his profession, and the acts of his life were related. There were different degrees among the priests, who were employed in metaphysical speculations, and who served the seven planets. Every planet had two sects of worshippers; each subdivided into seven classes. The first comprehended the priests, who worshipped, or served seven planets; the second, those who served six planets; the third, those who served five planets; the fourth, those who served four planets; the fifth, those who served three planets; the sixth, those who served two planets; the seventh,

[8] The stars are at this time represented in the East in their constellations, as may be seen in a fine MS. by Kazwini, in the library at the India House.—*Dr. Sprenger.*

[9] The account of the contents of the Pyramids is somewhat different in the extract of Makrizi. Every writer, indeed, seems to have enumerated as many marvellous things as his imagination could suggest.—*Dr. Sprenger.*

those who served one planet. The names[1] of these classes were inscribed on the sides of the sarcophagi; and within them were lodged books with golden leaves, upon which each priest had written a history of the past and a prophecy of the future. Upon the sarcophagi were, also, represented the manner, in which arts and sciences were performed, with a description of each process, and the object of it. The king assigned to every Pyramid a guardian: the guardian of the eastern Pyramid was an idol of speckled granite, standing upright, with a weapon like a spear in his hand; a serpent was wreathed round his head, which seized upon and strangled whoever approached, by twisting round his neck, when it again returned to its former position upon the idol. The guardian of the western Pyramid was an image made of black and white onyx, with fierce and sparkling eyes, seated on a throne, and armed with a spear; upon the approach of a stranger, a sudden noise was heard, and the image destroyed him. To the coloured (that is, the Third Pyramid) he assigned a statue, placed upon a pedestal, which was endowed with the power of entrancing every beholder till he perished. When every thing was finished, he caused the Pyramids to be haunted with living spirits; and offered up sacrifices to prevent the intrusion of strangers, and of all persons, excepting those, who by their conduct were worthy of admission. The author then says, that, according to the Coptic account, the following passage was inscribed, in Arabic, upon the Pyramids. "I, Surid, the king, have built these Pyramids, and have finished them in sixty-one years.[2] Let him, who comes after me, and imagines himself a king like me, attempt to destroy them in six hundred. To destroy is easier than to build. I have clothed them with silk; let him try to cover them with mats."

It is added, that the spirit of the northern Pyramid had been observed to pass around it in the shape of a beardless boy, with large teeth, and a sallow countenance; that the spirit of the western Pyramid was a naked woman, with large teeth, who seduced people into her power, and then made them insane, she was to be seen at mid-day and at sunset: and that the guardian of the coloured Pyramid, in the form of an old man, used to

[1] The names are given in the MS. of Masoudi, but they cannot be made out. —*Dr. Sprenger.*

[2] Makrizi says "in sixty years;" and states, that he had endeavoured to find this inscription, but in vain.—*Dr. Sprenger.*

scatter incense round the building with a thuribulum, like that used in Christian churches.[3]

The following story is related by Masoudi, in the "Akbar-Ezzeman."

Twenty men of the Faioum wished to examine the Pyramid. One of them was accordingly lowered down the well by means of a rope, which broke at the depth of one hundred cubits, and the man fell to the bottom; he was three hours falling. His companions heard horrible cries; and, in the evening, they went out of the Pyramid, and sat down before it to talk the matter over. The man, who was lost in the well, coming out of the earth, suddenly appeared before them, and uttered the exclamations— "Sak, Sak, Saka, Saka," which they did not understand; he then fell down dead, and was carried away by his friends. The above-mentioned words were translated by a man from Syad (Said,) as follows: "He, who meddles with, and covets what does not belong to him, is unjust."[4] Masoudi proceeds to relate, that, in a square chamber, some other explorers discovered in the lowest part of the Pyramid, a vase containing a quantity of fluid of an unknown quality. The walls of the chamber were composed of small square stones of beautiful colours; and a person, having put one of these stones in his mouth, was suddenly seized with a pain in his ears, which continued until he had replaced it. They also

[3] The Coptic account ends here. It appears from M. Quatremère's dissertation, that the traditions of the antient Egyptians were preserved by their descendants, the Copts, who were held in great respect by the Arabs. It is also said, that, in the reign of Ahmed Ben Touloun, who conquered Egypt about 260 A.H., a learned man, above one hundred years old, and of either Coptic or Nabathæan extraction, lived in Upper Egypt. This person had visited many countries, and was well informed of the antient history of Egypt, and was, by order of Ahmed Ben Touloun, examined before an assembly of learned Mahometans; and Masoudi's account of the Pyramids is said to have been given upon the authority of this learned man. Masoudi also mentions certain persons who were, by profession, guides to the Pyramids. It may be remarked, that the Arabian authors have given the same accounts of the Pyramids, with little or no variation, for above a thousand years; and that they appear to have repeated the traditions of the antient Egyptians, mixed up with fabulous stories and incidents, certainly not of Mahometan invention. The history, however, although evidently incorrect, yet seems as well worthy of credit, as the fables of Greek mythology, or as Homer's account of the heroes engaged in the Trojan war.—*Dr. Sprenger.*

[4] Makrizi has alluded to this story; and it is given at some length in MS. 9973, in the British Museum. This account has been taken from the latter document, on account of the bad condition of Masoudi's manuscript, but it has been carefully collated and compared with it.—*Dr. Sprenger.*

discovered, in a large hall, a quantity of golden coins put up in columns, every piece of which was of the weight of one thousand dinars. They tried to take the money, but were not able to move it. In another place they found the image of a sheik, made of green stone, sitting upon a sofa, and wrapped up in a garment. Before him were statues of little boys, whom he was occupied in instructing: they tried to take up one of these figures, but they were not able to move it. Having proceeded further to a quadrangular space, similar to that, which they had previously entered, they met with the image of a cock, made of precious stones, and placed upon a green column. Its eyes enlightened all the place; and, upon their arrival, it crowed, and flapped its wings. Continuing their researches, they came to a female idol of white stone, with a covering on her head, and lions of stone on each side, attempting to devour her, upon which they took to flight. This took place in the time of Yerid Ben Abdullah.[5]

In the "Golden Meadows," (9576 British Museum), the author, Masoudi, after adverting to the great size of the Pyramids, says, that they were inscribed with the unknown and unintelligible writings of people and of nations, whose names and existence have been long since forgotten. He then mentions, that the vertical height of the Great Pyramid was about four hundred cubits, and that its breadth was the same; and repeats the well-known tradition, that upon them were recorded the arts and sciences, various secrets, and knowledge, and also the sentence, "I have built them," &c.; he likewise narrates the story of the Mahometan king, who would have destroyed them, had he not found that the wealth of the whole kingdom would not have afforded him the means of doing so. The author says, that the Pyramids were built of squared stones of unequal size, and that they were the tombs of kings; that when one of these monarchs died, his body was placed in a sarcophagus of stone, called in Egypt and Syria, "Al Harm;" and that a Pyramid was built over it, with a subterraneous entrance, and a passage above one hundred cubits long; that the Pyramid was constructed in steps, which were built up and completed from the top to the bottom, and effaced when the whole was finished.

Masoudi, in his "Akbar-Ezzeman," also states, that when the Caliph Haroun Al Raschid was in Egypt, he wished to take down one of the Pyramids to see what it contained. He was told that

[5] Who was supposed to have been a king of Egypt.

it was impossible. He answered, that he was determined at least to open it; and accordingly made the chasm, (which was in the author's time visible), by means of fire and of vinegar, and of iron instruments, and of battering engines. He was at a great expense: and, having penetrated twenty cubits, he found a vessel filled with a thousand coins of the finest gold, each of which was a dinar in weight. When Haroun Al Raschid saw the gold, he ordered that the expenses, he had incurred, should be calculated, and the amount was found exactly equal to the treasure, which was discovered. He was at a loss to imagine how the cost of his operations could have been foretold, and how the money could have been placed exactly at the end of his excavation.

PAPYRUS FOUND IN THE MONASTERY OF ABOU HORMEIS.

TRANSLATED INTO ARABIC, 225 A.H.

It is said, that in a tomb at the monastery of Abou Hormeis, a body was found wrapped round with a cloth, and bearing upon the breast a papyrus, inscribed with antient Coptic characters, which could not be deciphered until, a monk, from the monastery of Al Kalmun in the Faioum, explained it as follows:[6] "In the first year of King Diocletian, an account was taken from a book, copied in the first year of King Philippus[7]—from an

[6] The story is related by Masoudi, but this relation of it by Al Kodhai is given, because he was a cadi in Egypt; and mentions the persons by whom the tradition had been handed down from former times.—*Dr. Sprenger*.

[7] Moses, of Chorene, seems to allude to this account when he mentions that Valarsaces sent to his brother Arsaces (the governor of Armenia), a learned man called Mariba to inquire into the antient history of Armenia. This person is supposed to have found, amongst the archives of Nineveh, a book, translated from Chaldaic into Greek by order of Alexander the Great, which contained historical records of the most remote antiquity. Valarsaces ordered them to be inscribed upon a column; and the author derived from this monument a considerable part of his history. Cedrenus also says, upon the authority of an apocryphal work ascribed by the Egyptians to Hermes, that Enoch, foreseeing the destruction of the earth, had inscribed the science of astronomy upon two pillars; the one composed of stone to resist the operation of water, and the other of brick to withstand that of fire. Cedrenus was a monk, and lived about 1050.—*Dr. Sprenger*.

inscription of great antiquity written upon a tablet of gold, which tablet[8] was translated by two brothers—Ilwa, and Yercha—at the request of Philippus, who asked them, how it happened that they could understand an inscription, which was unintelligible to the learned men in his capital? They answered, because they were descended from one of the antient inhabitants of Egypt, who was preserved with Noah in the ark, and who, after the flood had subsided, went into Egypt with the sons of Ham, and dying in that country left to his descendants, (from whom the two brothers received them), the books of the antient Egyptians, which had been written one thousand seven hundred and eighty-five years before the time of Philippus, nine hundred and forty-six years before the arrival of the sons of Ham in Egypt, and contained the history of two thousand three hundred and seventy-two years; and that it was from these books that the tablet was formed. The contents of the book were: 'We[9] have seen what the stars foretold; we saw the calamity descending from the heavens, and going out from the earth, and we were convinced that the waters would destroy the earth, with the inhabitants and plants. We told this to the King Surid Ben Shaluk: he built the Pyramids for the safety of us,[1] and also as tombs for himself and for his

[8] A French author remarks, that it is possible that in the two hundred and twenty-fifth year of the Hegra an Arabic version was found of a Greek translation from an antient MS., which may have related to celestial observations, and to the construction of the Pyramids; and also that the two larger Pyramids may, from their relative positions, have been called "eastern" and "western," and the Third, from the dark colour of the granite, termed "painted." He conceives that treasures, statues, and mummies, may have been found within them. He remarks, that the founder of the Great Pyramid is called Surid, son of Shaluk; of the Second, Herdjib; and of the Third, Kemses, son or nephew of Surid: an account which agrees with the Greek historians. He observes, that the entrances, which have been discovered, are on the northern sides, and about twelve metres above the bases of the Pyramids; but that in the time of the Caliph Al Mamoon, as the accumulation of rubbish must have been less, the subterraneous passages, mentioned by the Arabian historians, may have been more apparent; and he conceives that their accounts are, to a certain degree, founded on facts.

[9] Masoudi begins his narration of Surid (whose history he has taken from this document) by saying, that that monarch, son of Shaluk, king of Egypt, had a dream, which he imparted to the chief of the priests, and directed him to examine what the stars foretold, &c.—*Dr. Sprenger.*

[1] As there are two readings at this place, it does not appear that the meaning of the original was clearly known.—*Dr. Sprenger.*

household. When Surid died, he was buried in the eastern Pyramid; his brother Haukith, in the western; and his nephew Karwars, in the smaller — the lower part of which is built with granite, but the upper with a stone called Kedan.' The Pyramids are described to have had doors with subterraneous porticoes or passages one hundred and fifty cubits in length. The entrance into the eastern Pyramid is said to be on the side next the sea, and that of the strong Pyramid towards the Kiblah; and vast treasures and innumerable precious things are mentioned to have been enclosed in these buildings. Then the two brothers calculated what time had elapsed from the flood to the day when the translation was made by them for King Philip; and it appeared to be one thousand seven hundred and forty-one years, fifty-nine days, and twenty-three $\frac{59}{400}$ hours."

"In this manner were the Pyramids built. Upon the walls were written the mysteries of science, astronomy, geometry, physic, and much useful knowledge, which any person, who understands our writing, can read. The deluge was to take place when the heart of the Lion entered into the first minute of the head of Cancer, at the declining of the star. The other indications were, the Sun and Moon entering into the first minute of the head of Aries and Saturn, in the first degree and twenty-eight minutes of Aries; and Jupiter, in the twenty-ninth degree twenty-eight minutes of Pisces; and Hermes, *i.e.* Mercury, in the twenty-seventh minute of Pisces; the rising Moon, in the fifth degree and three minutes of the Lion."[3]

[2] Masoudi affirms, in the Akbar-Ezzeman, that he wrote his account of Surid from a Coptic modern history, entitled

تاريخ بوويه (يوويه) المصريين

[3] This statement was translated from the Coptic into Arabic 225 A.H., supposed to be four thousand three hundred and twenty-one years after the construction of the Pyramids. The astronomical observations are not inserted from an idea of their accuracy, but as they are expressed in the originals, although there is some difference between the MS. of Masoudi and that of Kodhai. Masoudi states, that Rawis Jupiter was in twenty-five minutes of Aries and Aphrodite; Venus in the twenty-ninth degree and three minutes of Pisces; that Saturn was in the Balance; and the rising Moon in the fifth day and five minutes of the Lion. An account of the appearance of the heavens when the waters subsided, is also included. — *Dr. Sprenger.*

MAKRIZI.

(DIED 845 A.H.)

His work on Egypt is No. 671 in Uri's Catalogue; and, in page 96, he observes, that besides many others there are eighteen Pyramids between Busir and Gizeh; that some of them are small and constructed with unburnt bricks, but that they are in general built with stone. A few are in steps or stages, but most of them have an inclined continuous form, and a smooth surface. A considerable number are situated at Gizeh opposite to Old Cairo Fostat; most of the smaller have been destroyed by Karakousch, (the vizier of Salah-eddin Youssef Ben Ayoub), who built with the materials Kela Gebel (the citadel), the walls of Cairo (Mesr), and the causeway with arches near Gizeh. He says, that there were various traditions respecting the three larger Pyramids at Gizeh, but that it was not known by whom, or for what purpose, they had been constructed. The author appears to have taken his remarks principally from "Abd Allatif," and then proceeds on the authority of Usted Ibrahim Ebn Wasyff Shah to give the account of Surid Ben Shaluk, related by Masoudi. He afterwards says, that the square of the base, and the height of the Great Pyramid, are five hundred cubits, each consisting of twenty-four inches;[6] that the four sides are equilateral, and that a line from the summit of the building down the centre of either of them would measure, if the Pyramid were perfect, five hundred cubits, but in its present state only four hundred and seventy. He states, that in a perfect state, the perpendicular height would be above four hundred cubits; that the base contains 500,000 square cubits. He considers that it is the most beautiful and extraordinary monument that was ever contrived, and that nothing can be compared with it. The excavation he attributes to the Caliph Al Mamoon, who, he says, ascended by a passage into a square chamber, where he found the sarcophagus which yet remains in it. The author then quotes from the fihrist (index) of Ibrahim Alwatwati al Warrak,[7]

[6] The MS. at Oxford is much defaced, but in a copy in the British Museum, 7317, these dimensions are said to be taken from Ali Ben Riswan, an Arab physician: Makrizi's whole account is indeed taken from other authorities.—*Dr. Sprenger.*

[7] According to M. Jomard's translation in the "Memoirs of the Institute," this author says, that a square chamber in the centre of the Great Pyramid, contains

that there was a great uncertainty about the history of Hermes of Babel; that according to some accounts he was one of the seven keepers in the temples,[3] whose business it was to guard the seven houses; and that he belonged to the temple of the planet Mercury, and acquired his name from his office, for Mercury, signifies in the Teradamian language, Hermes. He is also said to have reigned in Egypt, and to have had several children,[4] Taut, Aishm, Atrid, Koft. It is added, that he was renowned for his wisdom; and that he was buried in a building called Abou Hermes; and that his wife, or, according to other accounts, his son and successor, was buried in another; and that these two monuments were the Pyramids, and were called Haraman; that the height and breadth of the Great Pyramid were four hundred and eighty Hasheme cubits, and that the summit was a square of forty cubits, upon which an image had originally been placed.

He then cites from other authors, as follows:—

Mohammed Ben el Arabi, called also Mohiy Ed Din,—that the Pyramids were built by a people who believed in the metempsychosis, and that they were made use of in computing time.

Abul Sorur,—that the Pyramids were built by Hermes, or by kings, who were ambitious of the same distinction after their death, which they had possessed when alive.

Ben Matuy,—the discoveries are attributed to the Caliph Mamoon, and an account is given of the Pyramid of Meidoun.

Mohammed Ebn Abd Al Hokm,—that the Pyramids were constructed by Sheddad Ben Ad before the deluge; for that, if they had been built after that event had taken place, some positive and certain accounts of them would have remained.

Ibrahim Ben Ebn Wasyff Shah,—that the Pyramids were built by Surid, an antediluvian king, that they are defended by three guardians, and communicate with the Nile by means of a

a tomb made of polished stone, which had been painted; and also two statues, the one of a man holding a tablet of hieroglyphics, the other of a woman bearing a golden mirror; that between them was a vase containing a golden box full of liquid blood, closed up with bitumen; and that mummies of a man and of a woman, with idols and religious instruments, had been placed in the tomb.

[3] See Hammer; Purgstall, "Sur l'Influence Mahommedisme dans les Trois Premiers Siècles de l'Hegra" in the "Fundgrüben des Orients."—*Dr. Sprenger.*

[4] The names of the children of Hermes are written in the margin of the MS.—*Dr. Sprenger.*

canal. Historical events, and astronomical and medical treatises, were engraved upon them. The First was especially dedicated to history and astronomy; the Second to medical knowledge, and contained, in thirty chambers of granite, talismans, malleable glass, and other treasures; the priests were buried in sarcophagi made of granite, in the Third, and their annals were deposited with them. The stones of which the Pyramids are composed were fastened by iron rods through their centres, and by melted lead, and had been worked down from the top. These buildings were one hundred royal (five hundred common) cubits in height. They had all of them entrances forty cubits high; that of the eastern looked towards the east, of the Second to the west, and that of the Third to the south; that the entrances were one hundred cubits from the centre of their respective fronts, where the passages commenced.[5]

Abou Abd Allah Mohammed Ben Abdurakim Alkaisi,—that the Pyramids had quadrangular bases, and triangular sides; that they were eighteen in number; that the three largest were opposite to Fostat, and had bases five hundred cubits square, and were of the same height. That the largest (Haroun Youssef) was five hundred cubits in height, and had a circumference of two thousand. It was constructed with stones fifty cubits square. He also says, that the highest Pyramid was at the town of Haroun Misr; that it was like a mountain, and was built in five terraces, and was called "Meidoun."

Abou Yazid al Balkhi,—that an inscription was found upon a stone in the eastern Pyramid, which declared that, at the time when the two Pyramids were built, the Eagle was in conjunction with Gemini, 72,000 solar years before the Hegra.[6]

Abou Mohammed al Hassan Ben Ahmed Ben Yakub al Hamadani,—that the Pyramids were antediluvian, and that they resisted the force of the flood.

From another author, that the construction of the two

[5] M. Jomard imagines that the entrances are intended to be described as being forty cubits within the buildings, and that the passages were filled up with masonry for the distance of one hundred cubits.

[6] According to M. Jomard's translation of this author, Leo was in conjunction with Cancer. He remarks, that this account is very obscure; and says, that the traditions that the Pyramids were antediluvian buildings only prove their great antiquity, and that nothing certain was known about them; for that they have been attributed to Venephes, the fourth king of the first dynasty, and to Sensuphis, the second king of the fourth Memphite race.

Pyramids, to the westward of Fostat, was considered one of the wonders of the world; that they were squares of four hundred cubits, and faced the cardinal points. One was supposed to have been the tomb of Agathodæmon, the other that of Hermes, who reigned in Egypt for one thousand years; both of them were said to have been inspired persons, and to have been endowed with prophetic powers. That according to other accounts, these monuments were the tombs of Sheddad Ben Ad, and of other monarchs who conquered Egypt.

Ebn Ofeir, that it was reported that Sheddad Ben Ad built the Pyramids.

In the "Manahiy al Fikr," by Ialal Uldin Mohammed Ben Ibrahim Alwatwati al Warrak, the same tradition is mentioned, but the names have the terminations of Hebrew plurals; Sheddak (Sheddad) Ben Adim, Ben Nerdeshir, Ben Cophtim, Ben Mizraim; and Sheddad is said to be an Egyptian. According to the testimony of the same author, (907 in Uri's Catalogue), and to that of Abou Mohammed Mustafa (785 Uri's Catalogue), the Adites worshipped the moon.

In an account written about 800 A.H., it is said, that Sheddad Ben Ad reigned over the whole world; that the Adites were very powerful, and peculiarly favoured by the Almighty; that they were giants, and endowed with supernatural strength, and exclaimed, "Who is stronger than we?" It is stated, that the Deity replied, "Do you not know that God, who created you, is stronger?" But that, notwithstanding repeated expostulations and the warnings of the Prophet Hud, sent for their admonition, they continued rebellious, and were destroyed by the Almighty.[8]

Abou Szalt[9] of Spain, says, in his "Risaleh" (Memoirs), that it is evident, from their works, that the antient Egyptians possessed great knowledge and science, particularly in geometry and astronomy; and mentions, in support of this opinion, the Pyramids and Barabi,[1] which had excited the admiration and astonishment of all beholders: "For what," he asks, "can be more surprising than these immense buildings, consisting of enormous blocks, with equilateral triangular sides, four hundred and sixty cubits in height, and which, besides the beauty of their proportions,

[8] This is mentioned in the 89th chapter of the Koran.—*Dr. Sprenger.*

[9] This author is mentioned by Edrisi.—*Dr. Sprenger.*

[1] This appears to be an Egyptian word adopted by the Arabs.

possess a solidity, that neither tempests nor time can destroy?" The author then quotes the verses of Motanebbi, mentioned by Ebn Al Werdi;[2] and also says, that the Pyramids were supposed to have been the tombs of antient kings, who were as desirous of posthumous glory as they had been of renown during their existence, and who intended, by these buildings, to transmit their names to remote posterity.

He mentions, that when the Caliph Al Mamoon arrived in Egypt, he ordered the Pyramids to be opened, and that an excavation was accordingly made in one of them with great labour and expense, which, at length, disclosed an ascending narrow passage, dreadful to look at, and difficult to pass. At the end of it was a quadrangular chamber, about eight cubits square, and within it a sarcophagus. The lid was forced open, but nothing was discovered excepting some bones completely decayed by time; upon which the caliph declined any further examination, as the expenses had been very great, particularly in provisions for the workmen. The author then observes, that it has been mentioned, that Hermes, called Trismegistus, and, in Hebrew, Enoch, having ascertained, from the appearances of the stars, that the deluge would take place, built the Pyramids to contain his treasures, and books of science and knowledge, and other matters, worth preserving from oblivion and ruin; but that it has also been said, that the founder of the Pyramids was either Surid Ben Shaluk, or Sheddad Ben Ad; that the Copts did not believe that the Amalekites came to Egypt, but that the Pyramids were built by Surid in consequence of a dream, in which he saw appearances in the heavens, which portended the flood; that he built them in six months, and covered them with coloured silk, and placed upon them the inscription already mentioned,—"I have built," &c. He likewise says, that the surfaces of the two Pyramids were covered with inscriptions from the top to the bottom, and that the lines were close to one another, but almost erased; but that it was not positively known who built them, nor what was the meaning of the inscriptions; in short, that every thing connected with them was mysterious, and the traditions respecting them various and contradictory; at the same time, that they commanded such admiration and astonishment, that they were actually worshipped. He adds, that the caliph ordered his people to ascend the Great Pyramid, which they accomplished in

[2] Ebn Al Werdi's writings have been translated by Frehn.—*Dr. Sprenger.*

three hours, and found at the summit a space sufficient for eight camels to lie down, and upon it a body, wrapped up in cloths, so much decomposed by time, that scarcely any part of them remained, except an embroidery of gold. A hall was likewise mentioned in this Pyramid, whence three doors led to as many chambers; that the doors were ten cubits long and five broad, and were composed of marble slabs, beautifully put together, and inscribed with unknown characters. They are said to have resisted their efforts for three days; but being at length forced open, three marble columns were discovered at the distance of ten cubits, supporting the images of three birds in flames of fire. Upon the first, was that of a dove, formed of green stone; upon the second, that of a hawk, of yellow stone; and upon the third, the image of a cock, of red stone. Upon moving the hawk, the door which was opposite moved, and upon lifting it up, the door was raised; and the same connexion existed between the other images and doors. In one of the chambers they found three couches, formed of a shining stone, and upon them three bodies; each body was shrouded in three garments, and over their heads were tablets inscribed with unknown characters. The other chamber contained arches of stone, and upon them chests of the same material, full of arms and of other instruments. The length of one of the swords was seven spans; and the coats of mail measured twelve spans. All these things were brought out, and the doors were closed, as at first, by order of the caliph. The number of the Pyramids are said to have been eighteen; the three greatest were opposite to Fostat; and the base of the largest was a square of five hundred cubits. A sarcophagus is also said to have been found in the Pyramid, covered with a lid of stone, and filled with gold; and upon the cover was written, in Arabic characters, "Abou Amad built this Pyramid in 1000 days."

The caliph is likewise said to have found a hollow image of a man made of green stone, and covered with a stone like an emerald, which contained a body in golden armour, a sword of inestimable value, and a ruby as large as an egg. According to some accounts, the hollow case of green stone was to be seen at the palace at Cairo in 511 A.H.[4]

Hundreds of books have been written on the mathematics of the Great Pyramid. but only one reveals the very foundation of its structure by using provable measures. It is called *The Source of Measures* by J. Ralston Skinner. Skinner found that the actual measures of the Great Pyramid are based on the following theorim using pi (π). What follows is the six page Introduction to this important work, made available for those wishing to explore the subject further.

THE SOURCE OF MEASURES

INTRODUCTION.

THE following, in place of a work, strictly speaking, is rather an essay or study. It is like the study of an artist, where it comprehends many details in outline going to make up a whole, yet unfinished and subject to change, here and there, as the blending of details may prove inharmonious or incongruous to the general scope of the design. Unlike such a study, however, others can join in the labor of completing the task; and it is hoped that it may prove an incentive to that end.

The whole constitutes a series of developments, based upon the use of geometrical elements, giving expression in a numerical value. These elements are found in the work of the late John A. Parker, of the city of New York, setting forth *his* discovery (but, in fact, the rediscovery) of *a* quadrature value of the circle. Upon this one, that of Peter Metius, of the sixteenth century, seems to be a variation.

Mr. Parker makes use of an element of measure of the equilateral triangle, by which, as a *least unit* of measure, to express the measure of the elements of a circle in terms of the numerical value of a square: so that, as a conclusion, a square of 81 to the side, or 6561 in area, shall contain a circle whose area equals 5153; or, rectifying the circumference, a diameter of 6561 shall have a circumference of $5153 \times 4 = 20612$.

Let it be understood that the question of value of the quadrature, whether by Mr. Parker, or by Metius, as to whether it is the expression of exactitude of relation, does not arise; nor is it, save incidentally, pertinent to the subject-matter in hand. While this work thus is relieved of any necessity of examination into the question of the possibility of what is called "*the quadrature*," or "*the squaring of the circle*," nevertheless, it is necessary to a proper understanding of the whole that some, to many persons very dry, details of Mr. Parker's construction of his quadrature should be set forth in the very commencement. Incidentally, however, it is thought that the matters established herein, as having a direct relation to the *holy things of God, as laid down in Scripture*, will force an inquiry, on the part of devout people, into the abstract question of "*the quadrature*," both as received and as set forth by Parker and by Metius; and also into the question of any special value of the quadrature by Parker, as related to the generally accepted one.

One development is as follows: The numerical value, 20612, of a circumference is made use of to derive from it a *unit of measure* for *linear*, *superficial*, and *solid* measure. Thus, as a common unit of measure is the edge of one of the faces of a cube, and as there are twelve edges to the cube, the division of 20612 by 12 is the distribution of this value onto these 12 edges; so that the quotient, which is 1717.66+, is that unit of measure, which is, however it may be used, convertible into circular, and again, back into the geometrical elements whence derived. And this is obtained by the special numerical value, 171766+, the one-twelfth of 20612, whether, as a fact, it be used as a whole or as a part, as 1.71766+. Now, as a fact, 1.71766+ of the *British foot* is the ancient *cubit value;* hence, the whole scheme thus far displayed has been practically utilized, inasmuch as 20612 is thus seen to be of the value of *British inches*, while its derivative of 171766+, so divided or scaled as to represent 1.71766+, is the ancient cubit.

This is confirmed from the fact of restoration, by means of these numerical values, of the great pyramid of Egypt, in terms of the British measures thereof made of late years.

Another development is that, by a variation on the use of these numerical values, taken systematically, not empirically, a diameter value to a circumference value of 6 is found, which is discovered to be the basis of the Hindu method for the calculation of tables of *sines* and *cosines*, *tangents* and *cotangents*, and of the *orbits* of planetary bodies; which variation, as an enlargement of the above values, on application, is found to give the exactitude of the pyramid measures, agreeably to the design of the architect, thus again coupling a modern with an ancient use.

Another development is that the British system of *long* and *land* measures is discovered to contain an occult or obscure system of *time* calculations, based on the factor 6, by which it is seen that the entirety of the British measures rests upon these anciently developed elements, and thus is, in fact, but a phase of the Hindu system. The factor 6 is the base of the *acre* and *mile* measure, running up from the *inch* and *foot*, and the equivalent of the base side of the pyramid (which is a diameter value to a circumference of 24) is the side of a square, divided into four equal parts of $\overline{6\times6}$ each, in terms of the British foot, and necessarily the inch; hence the advanced measures, as far as the mile, are thus involved. But while this is so, the means of obtaining this pyramid measure is through use of the Parker elements; hence the Parker elements are thus connected with the whole range of British measures.

But the greatest development is that the entire system seems to have been anciently regarded as one resting in nature, and one which was adopted by nature, or God, as the *basis* or *law* of the exertion practically of creative power—i. e., it was the *creative design*, of which creation was practically the application. This seems to be established by the fact that, under the system set forth, measures of *planetary times* serve co-ordinately as measures of the *size* of planets, and of the peculiarity of their shapes—i. e., in the extension of their equatorial and polar diameters, in terms of the British measures, or the cubit measures arising, as stated, from the forms of Mr. Parker.

The true study of the Deity by man being in the observation of His works, the discovery of a fundamental *creative law* (in numbers and measures), as regards His works, of as wide and comprehensive grasp as shown, would locate the substance of such a discovery as the practical real tangible link between God and man, as that by which man can in a measure realize the actually existing working qualities of God, just, speaking most reverentially, as he would those of a fellow-man—as, say, of a mason, or of a carpenter; thus revealing tangible existence, likeness, relationship, and, remotely, companionship. Such a link, once found, would constitute a base for superstructures of recognition, praise, worship, and copy. As a fact, this system seems to underlie the whole Biblical structure, as a foundation for its *ritualism*, and for its display of the works of the Deity in the way of *architecture*, by use of the sacred unit of measure in the Garden of Eden, the Ark of Noah, the Tabernacle, and the Temple of Solomon.

Such seem to be the characteristics of development from the elements of quadrature of the late Mr. Parker. The extent to which the development is made so as to compel a mental assent, must be tested, of course, through the contents of the work. There is no disposition on the part of the author to make any assertion as to the strength of his work. What he has done has been done to the best of his ability, and he believes that a studiously careful reading of the work done, will be that, and alone that, upon which any fair criticism can be based.

Since, after all, all matters of science subordinate themselves to any one by which man can arrive to a realizable knowledge of God, all things in this book are of poor value in every other regard, comparatively, save as they lead up just to this kind or condition of knowledge. Such being the case, the following statements may be made as *introductory:*

(1.) The "*Quadrature of the Circle*," by John A. Parker, sets forth the integral relation of diameter to circumference of a circle as 6561 to 20612, derived from area computations, viz: area of square being 6561, area of inscribed circle is 5153; and diameter being 6561, rectification of circumference is $5153 \times 4 = 20612$.

(2.) It appears that nature was regarded as making use of this numerical relation, as a law or application of numbers to measures, by which to construct the mechanical properties of the universe; so regulating the times of the planets that they should move by a numerical system such that by it the measure of their shapes was to be obtained in a definite class or scale of measures adapted to the same system: so that movement should co-ordinate with size under the same system.

(3.) However man obtained knowledge of the practical measure, *the British inch*, by which nature was thought to adjust the planets in size to harmonize with the notation of their movements, it seems he did obtain it, and esteemed its possession as the means of his realization of the Deity—that is, he approached so nearly to a conception of a Being having a mind like his own, only infinitely more powerful, as to be able to realize *a law of creation* established by that Being, which must have existed prior to any creation (kabbalistically called the *Word*). The knowledge thus gained was simply that of the measure spoken of with its uses, in connection with the geometrical elements from whence it sprung.

(4.) This knowledge as to its origin, interpretation, and use, became somehow that of a *caste* condition. As such it was most sedulously concealed, and when set forth it was only in a secret or very obscured way. One way of setting it forth was by *hieroglyphic writing*. This method is the burden of the Hebrew Bible. Another way was by *architectural display*. The greatest ever made was in the great pyramid of Egypt; the next greatest seems to have been in the temple of Solomon.

(5.) It is thought the restoration of this pyramid agreeably to the design of the architect, will afford the means of translation of the hieroglyphic meanings of the Hebrew Bible, as, on hypothesis, the one was written and the other built to set forth the same natural problems.

The first step, therefore, necessary to the deciphering of the hieroglyphic or symbolic meanings of the Hebrew Bible, is the restoration of the great pyramid after its architectural conception. This is the chief burden of this work; and it is thought that the intent of the architect has been so far recovered as to justify publication. Secondarily, it is to be shown that the Temple was but another architectural style of setting forth the same measures with the pyramid. The balance of the matters, condensed as much as possible into brief outline, chiefly serves to exemplify the method of Biblical application of the pyramid system. This balance is noted here and there in the text, and is contained in the appendices. It serves to relieve the dry details of figures and calculations, to show related connections, and is hoped to excite interest in the whole subject, and to stimulate those who may read, to an earnest effort in the further prosecution of this subject so fascinating in its elucidations.

The relation of 6561 : 20612 is both in the pyramid structure and in the Bible coupled with the form 113 : 355. Some connections between the two will be shown, but what the exact basic relations between them were, as anciently recognized, remains to be discovered.

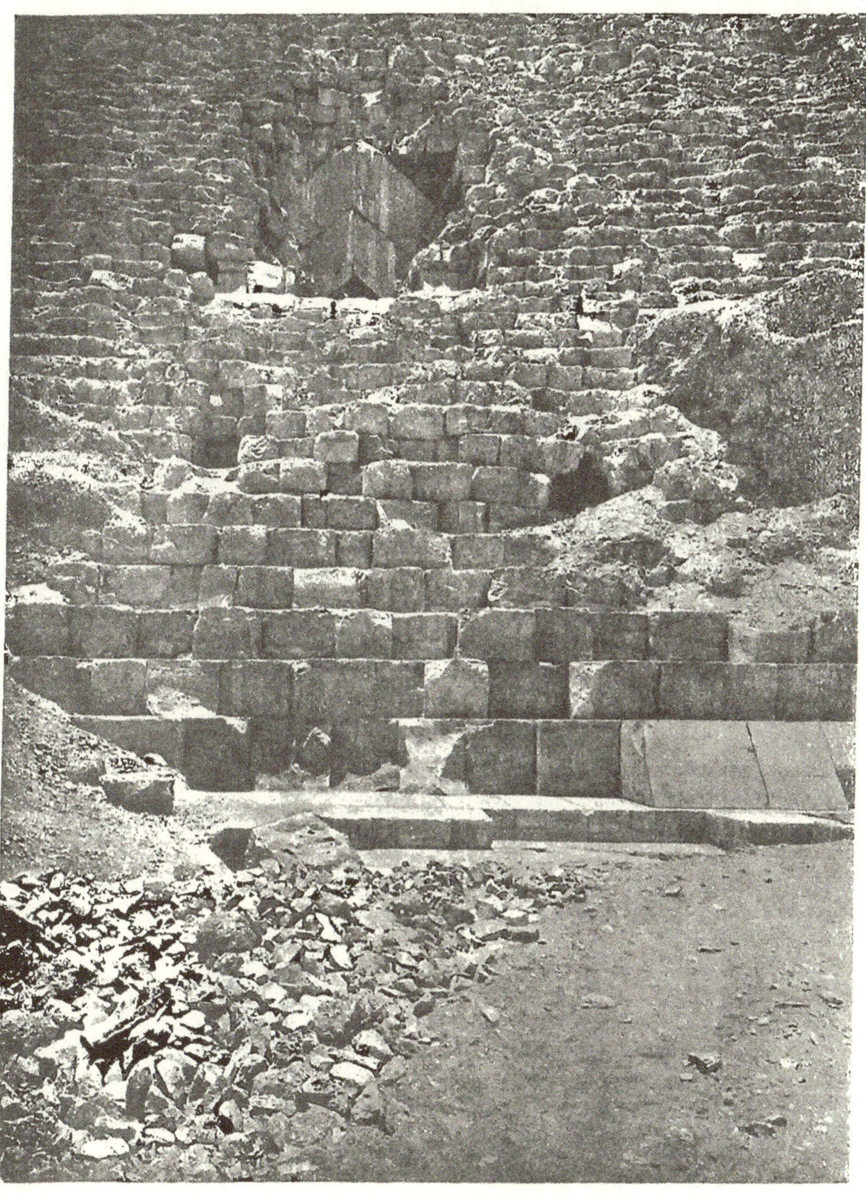

The MIDDLE of the NORTH BASE of the GREAT PYRAMID of Gizeh; showing the angle-stones above the Entrance, the casing-stones, and the entrance of Al Mamoun's forced passage.

Col. Howard Vyse's historical CASING-STONES in the middle of the north base of the Great Pyramid of Gizeh; alongside of which stands Hadji Ali Gabri, whose father, when a boy, was in the employment of Col. Howard Vyse during his extensive operations at the Pyramids in 1837 A.D

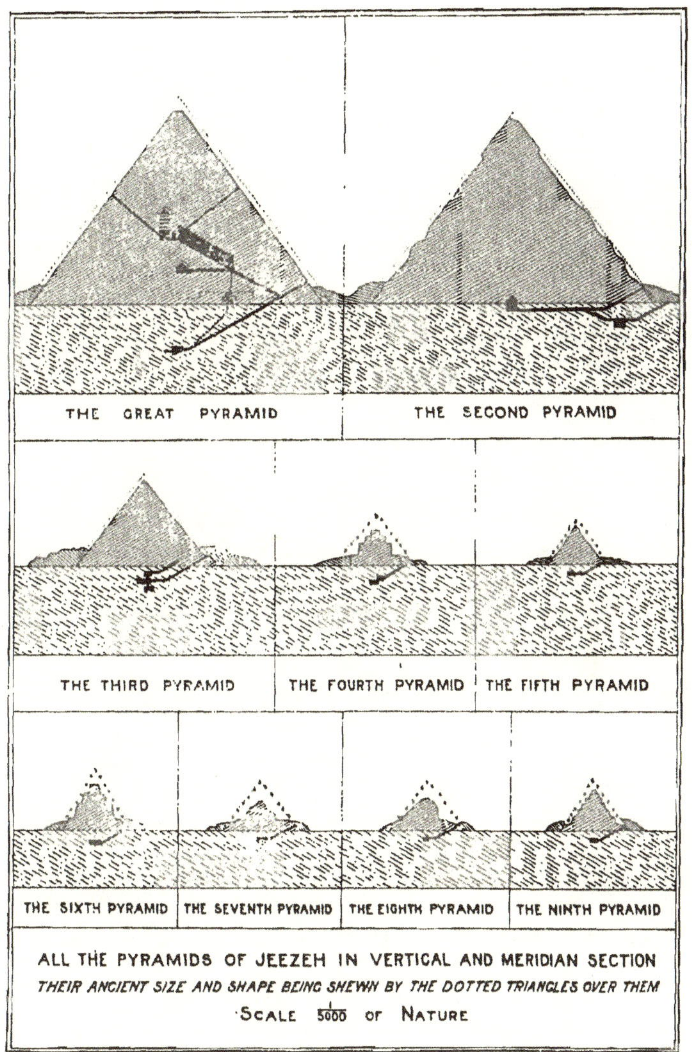

ALL THE PYRAMIDS OF JEEZEH IN VERTICAL AND MERIDIAN SECTION

THEIR ANCIENT SIZE AND SHAPE BEING SHEWN BY THE DOTTED TRIANGLES OVER THEM

SCALE $\frac{1}{5000}$ OF NATURE

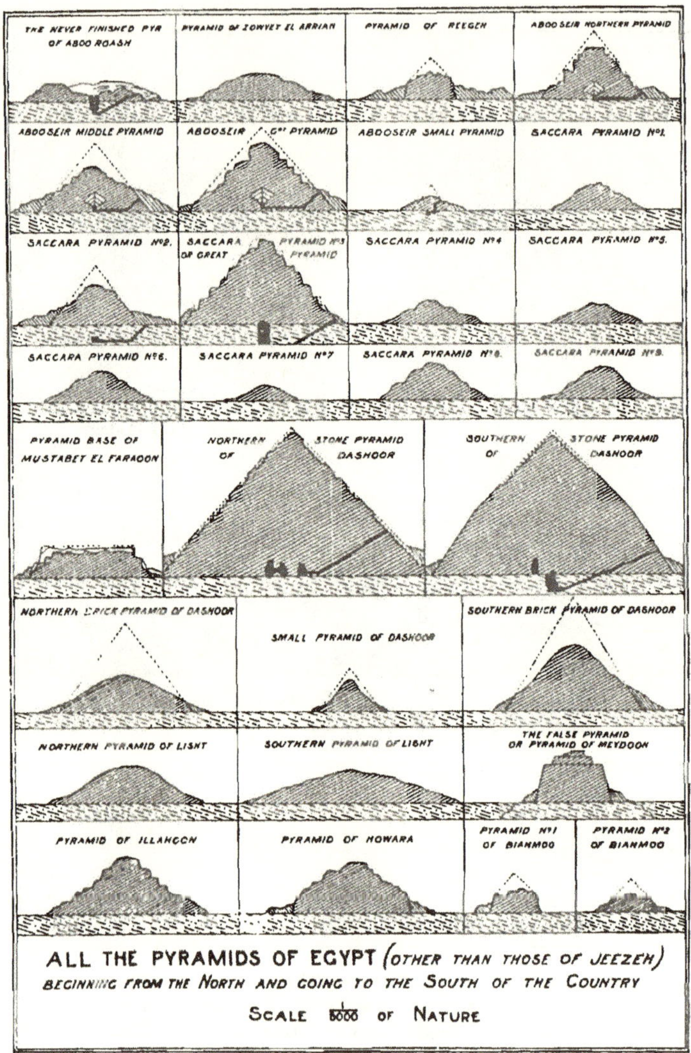

ALL THE PYRAMIDS OF EGYPT (OTHER THAN THOSE OF JEEZEH)
BEGINNING FROM THE NORTH AND GOING TO THE SOUTH OF THE COUNTRY
SCALE $\frac{1}{5000}$ OF NATURE

The GREAT PYRAMID of Gizeh, from the sand-hills above Mena House Hotel; showing the terminus of the carriage-drive which connects Cairo with the Pyramids.

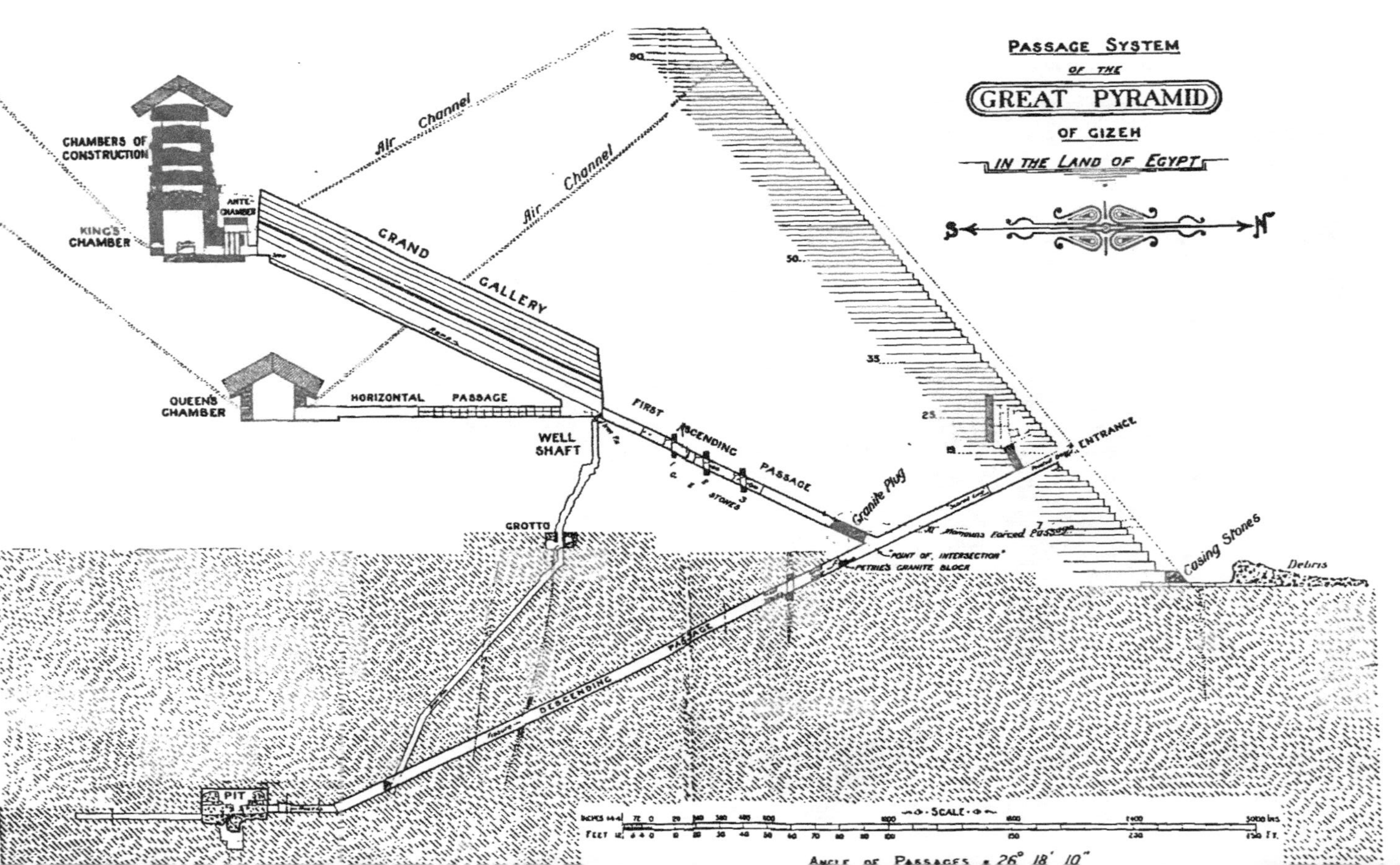

PASSAGE SYSTEM
OF THE
GREAT PYRAMID
OF GIZEH
IN THE LAND OF EGYPT
S
N
CHAMBERS OF CONSTRUCTION
KING'S CHAMBER
ANTE-CHAMBER
Air Channel
Air Channel
GRAND GALLERY
QUEENS CHAMBER
HORIZONTAL PASSAGE
WELL SHAFT
GROTTO
FIRST ASCENDING PASSAGE
STONES
Granite Plug
ENTRANCE
Mamouns Forced Passage
POINT OF INTERSECTION
PETRIE'S GRANITE BLOCK
Casing Stones
Debris
DESCENDING PASSAGE
PIT
90
50
35
25
SCALE
ANGLE OF PASSAGES = 26° 18' 10"

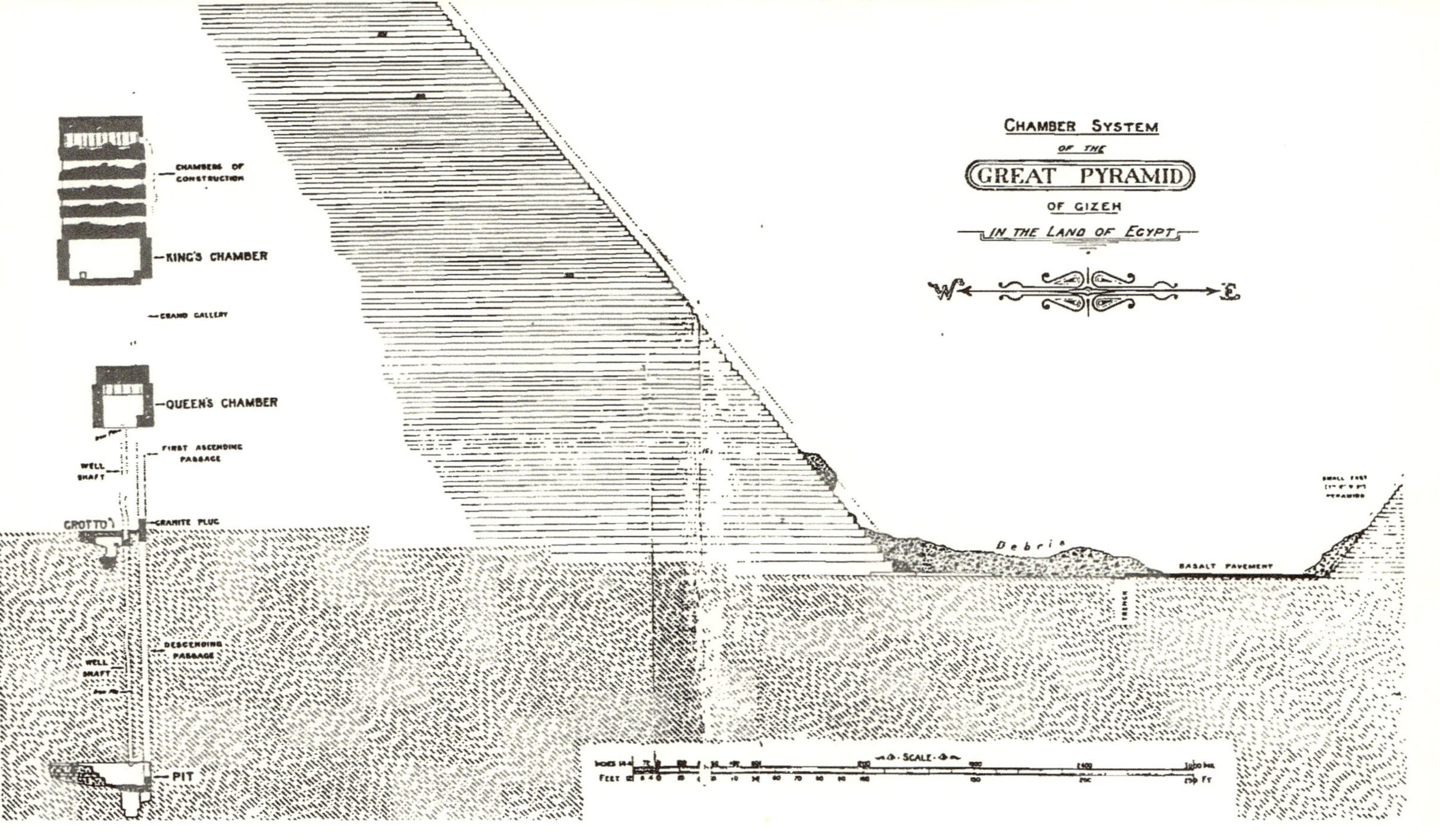

CHAMBER SYSTEM
OF THE
GREAT PYRAMID
OF GIZEH
IN THE LAND OF EGYPT
W
E
CHAMBERS OF CONSTRUCTION
KING'S CHAMBER
GRAND GALLERY
QUEEN'S CHAMBER
FIRST ASCENDING PASSAGE
WELL SHAFT
GROTTO
GRANITE PLUG
DESCENDING PASSAGE
WELL SHAFT
PIT
Debris
BASALT PAVEMENT
TRENCH
SCALE
INCHES
FEET

www.ingramcontent.com/pod-product-compliance
Lightning Source LLC
Chambersburg PA
CBHW031853090426
42741CB00005B/473

* 9 7 8 1 5 8 5 0 9 4 6 4 6 *